CW01676633

The Gloucestershire Warwickshire Steam Railway Past & Present

John Whitehouse

Past and Present

A Past and Present
Limited Edition of 360 copies
Published 24 May 2019

A PAST and PRESENT Companion

The Gloucestershire Warwickshire Steam Railway Past and Present

Honeybourne to Cheltenham

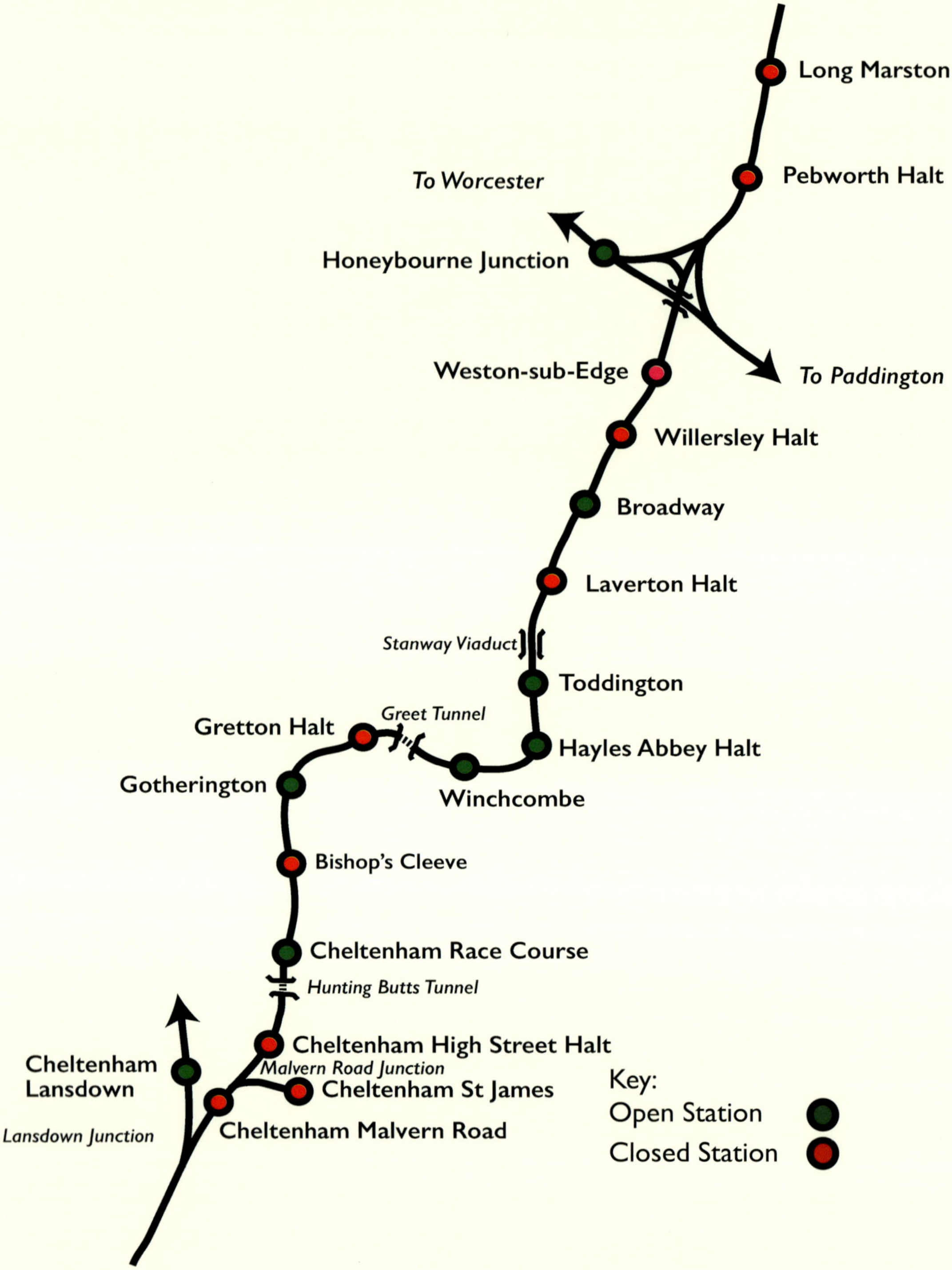
Long Marston
Pebworth Halt
To Worcester
Honeybourne Junction
To Paddington
Weston-sub-Edge
Willersley Halt
Broadway
Laverton Halt
Stanway Viaduct
Toddington
Gretton Halt
Greet Tunnel
Hayles Abbey Halt
Gotherington
Winchcombe
Bishop's Cleeve
Cheltenham Race Course
Hunting Butts Tunnel
Cheltenham High Street Halt
Cheltenham Lansdown
Malvern Road Junction
Cheltenham St James
Lansdown Junction
Cheltenham Malvern Road
Key:
Open Station
Closed Station

A PAST and PRESENT Companion

The Gloucestershire Warwickshire Steam Railway Past and Present

Honeybourne to Cheltenham

John Whitehouse

'Modified Hall' No. 7903 *Foremarke Hall* departs from Toddington in September 2016 *JW*

In loving memory of John & Doris Bate – they made this possible

© John Whitehouse 2019

All rights reserved. No part of this publication may be reproduced, stored in a retrieval system or transmitted, in any form or by any means, electronic, mechanical, photocopying, recording or otherwise, without prior permission in writing from Past & Present Ltd.

First published in 2019

British Library Cataloguing in Publication Data

A catalogue record for this book is available from the British Library.

ISBN 978 1 85895 293 2 (Hardback)
978 1 85895 292 5 (Softback)

Past & Present Publishing Ltd
The Trundle
Ringstead Road
Great Addington
Kettering
Northants NN14 4BW

Tel/Fax: 01536 330588
email: sales@nostalgiacollection.com
Website: www.nostalgiacollection.com

Printed and bound in the Czech Republic

Acknowledgements

In order to complete this volume it has been necessary to impose upon the time of many people, and the fact that all who have been so charged have responded magnificently to my pleadings is a testament to their generosity. Once again, Tony Bowles of the Restoration & Archiving Trust has been a notable supporter in providing key material. The same sentiments apply to David Postle of the Kidderminster Railway Museum who, whilst under the considerable stress of project-managing the building of the new Bridgnorth station, still found the time to deal with my requests for material. Bryan Nicholls provided access to his wonderful private museum at Gotherington West, as well as providing material from his private collection. Keith Smith of Middleton Press very kindly introduced me to contacts of his who had access to rare images of certain locations.

My grateful thanks go to the Gloucestershire Warwickshire Steam Railway for allowing me the necessary lineside access, and moreover to Ian Crowder and Graham Radband of the GWSR, for opening a good number of doors through which I could poke my camera. A special mention, too, for Ann Greenwood of Cheltenham's Clifton Diocese, who made my day by solving the identity of a now long-lost church tower behind St James station, a mystery that had been troubling me for a good while (see page 118).

My thanks, too, to all the photographers who have made their work available to me, and who are acknowledged in the caption details. Without their support, there would have been no book!

And finally to Richard Tuplin, who again took on the task of proofreading the text, and in so doing made many positive suggestions to improve the finished product. I am truly grateful for that input, so all I can add is that any errors that remain are entirely of my own making. I am pleased to add that Richard is recovering well from the ordeal!

Bibliography and Author's note

An Illustrated History of the Stratford on Avon to Cheltenham Railway by Audie Baker (Irwell Press, 1994; ISBN 1-871608-62-7)
Stratford-upon-Avon to Cheltenham – Country Railway Routes by Vic Mitchell and Keith Smith (Middleton Press, 1998; ISBN 978-1-901706-25-3)
Lost Railways of Gloucestershire by Stan Yorke (Countryside Books, 2009; ISBN 978-1-84674-163-0)
Various issues of 'The Cornishman', the house magazine of the GWSR

There is a potential conflict with the initials GWR, so to clarify the situation all references to 'GWR' relates to the historic Great Western Railway, which operated between 1833 and 1948, and those to 'GWSR' relate to the Gloucestershire Warwickshire Steam Railway Limited, formed in 1981.

Contents

Introduction

'The Honeybourne Line' is the name given to the route constructed by the Great Western Railway (GWR), not just to connect Honeybourne and Cheltenham Spa, but also as part of a larger strategic plan to provide the company with a faster route from Birmingham to the South West that avoided the need to exercise running rights over the metals of its arch-rival, the Midland Railway. From Honeybourne the route ran south via Toddington and Winchcombe to join the GWR's existing Cheltenham branch line from Gloucester, which operated into Cheltenham Spa (St James) station; this branch, which had opened in 1847, connected with the Midland Railway at Lansdown Junction.

Today, any mention of 'The Honeybourne Line' will likely generate a blank look on the faces of many, but refer to 'The Gloucestershire Warwickshire Steam Railway' (GWSR) and the reaction will be totally different, as the heritage line is now an integral part of the local community and an important asset to the Cotswold's tourist industry.

The line was surveyed to run close to the Cotswold Hills with gentle curves and gradients to allow ease of operation. It is laid on clay, which over time has caused problems with settlement and stability, as evidenced by some significant landslips (of which more later). From Honeybourne the line climbs towards a summit at Broadway, before a gentle descent to the site of Laverton Halt. A short climb to Toddington then follows, after which there are undulating but easy grades through to Winchcombe. After a spike at the south end of Gretton Tunnel, the line follows a falling gradient through Gotherington, Bishop's Cleeve and Cheltenham Race Course into Cheltenham, where around a mile of climbing at 1 in 106 is followed by an approximately half-mile descent at 1 in 105 into Malvern Road station. Except where specifically quoted here, the prevailing gradient is between 1 in 150 and 1 in 200.

Opened incrementally, commencing with the section from Honeybourne to Broadway on 1 August 1904, the final part of the route, the connection at Cheltenham Spa, was first used by revenue-earning traffic from August 1906. The completion of the line, which was always intended as a fast through route as apposed to a local line, together with the opening of the North Warwickshire Line in 1908 and the provision of a chord from Honeybourne East Loop to West Loop Junction, thereby creating an avoiding line for Honeybourne, finally accomplished the GWR's strategic plan.

The route allowed fast expresses, such as the

This is the historic first public passenger train departure from Broadway in 58 years, as No 7903 *Foremarke Hall* eases away from the station on 30 March 2018. *JW*

famous daily return Wolverhampton to Penzance service, named 'The Cornishman' from 1952, to benefit from quicker journey times. Freight services, too, could offer improved connections between the East Midlands and South Wales, particularly for coal and iron ore workings. Local traffic, however, was not abundant; when the line first opened trains were operated by GWR steam railmotors, essentially a passenger coach with an internal boiler. Later, auto-trains using small '1400' Class or '6400' Class pannier tanks became the norm, operating with either one or two coaches. The local services were known affectionately as 'The Coffee Pot', which is thought to originally have been a reference to the vertical boiler in the railmotor vehicles, which resembled such a domestic appliance.

Goods facilities were provided at most of the stations along the line, and were well used by fruit growers, for which the Vale of Evesham is well known, and local farmers, all of whom used the railway to get their perishable products quickly to the principal markets in London, Bristol and Birmingham.

The majority of stations opened with the line, the exceptions being Willersey Halt (October 1904), Hayles Abbey (September 1928), Cheltenham Race Course (March 1912), Cheltenham (High Street Halt) (October 1908) and Cheltenham Malvern Road (March 1908). Their closure followed a similar pattern, with most being shut upon the withdrawal of the local passenger service on 7 March 1960. The exceptions were Gotherington (June 1955), Cheltenham Race Course (March 1968, reopened March 1971 and closed again August 1976), Cheltenham (High Street Halt) (April 1917) and Cheltenham Malvern Road (January 1966).

Between these times the line functioned as planned, providing the GWR with an opportunity to run a mix of services through two World Wars, as well as fluctuating economic climates. However, the growth of road usage for both commercial and domestic purposes in the early 1950s began to chip away at the railway's core markets. Passengers and freight increasingly switched to road transport, which not only offered much greater flexibility but also personal choice as to when and where to travel.

Railway cuts loomed, and it was of little surprise that the local passenger service between Honeybourne and Cheltenham Spa was withdrawn with effect from 7 March 1960, with the associated station closures as detailed above. Local goods traffic continued for a while, but it, too, had been lured away by road hauliers, and slowly but surely all the goods yards were closed, with Toddington the last to go on 2 January 1967. Through freight traffic continued, and indeed the West Loop Yard, which had opened in 1960 especially to deal with heavy iron ore trains, survived in part through to 1981.

Express workings continued for a few years, but scheduled steam-hauled workings ceased in September 1965. The last timetabled working to use the route, a DMU-operated Leamington Spa to Gloucester service,

The late-afternoon glint at 'Chicken Curve' illuminates No D6948 as it threads around the curve heading for Broadway on 28 October 2018. *JW*

was withdrawn on 23 March 1968. Despite all this, the line continued to be used for diverted passenger services into the 1970s.

In an interesting turn of events, British Rail (BR) actually reopened Cheltenham Race Course station for the March 1971 Gold Cup meeting, and it was used soon afterwards by the Royal Train, when HM The Queen visited Cheltenham the following month. The station continued to be used each year for race meetings up to 1976, when the programme of special trains for the Gold Cup meeting of that year proved to be the last due to the subsequent closure of the line some months later. However, as history shows, race-day specials were to return, details of which are described later in this book.

In the years preceding closure there had been conflicting rumours concerning the future of the line. While many concerned the abandoning and lifting of the route, there was one suggesting that BR was looking at the line for high-speed HST workings, and even later still, in the preservation era, potential reopening as a relief route to the crowded former Midland cross-country line between Birmingham and Bristol.

However, most of these stories were finally consigned to oblivion when on 25 August 1976 a Toton to Severn Tunnel Junction freight, hauled by 'Peak' Class 45 No 45076, derailed on the Toddington side of the B4632 road bridge (see page 65), on the approach to the site of Winchcombe station. Fortunately the wagons did not leave the track until they had passed over the road bridge, but substantial track damage resulted. The consequence was that the line was closed on 1 November 1976.

The track was lifted during 1979, by which time most of the infrastructure had long been removed, most going after the withdrawal of the passenger service in 1960. Remarkably, Toddington station building, signal box and goods shed all survived, as did the road-level booking office at Cheltenham Race Course together with the goods sheds at Broadway and Winchcombe. Gotherington station building was also a notable survivor, as it had already passed into private ownership after its closure in 1955.

The progressive rundown of the line had already galvanised local opposition to closure, which resulted in the formation of the Gloucestershire Warwickshire Railway Society, ironically a week before the Winchcombe derailment, whose aims were either to prevent closure or, if that could not be avoided, preserve the line for future use. The society became a trust one year later, which continued in its proactive work of reopening the line. When track-lifting commenced in 1979 the focus changed to ensuring that the trackbed was preserved.

With the track lifted, behind-the-scenes progress continued, culminating with BR granting the trust a lease over part of the Toddington site in March 1981, followed a few months later by the arrival of the first items of rolling stock (see page 43). Perhaps of even more importance, BR had indicated a willingness to sell the trackbed, and in response the Gloucestershire Warwickshire Steam Railway plc (GWSR) was incorporated in August of that year in order to raise the necessary capital.

There is an anomaly with the 'Gloucestershire Warwickshire' name, as the railway does not at any point enter Warwickshire. Indeed, until the extension to Broadway was completed in March 2018, the railway operated exclusively in Gloucestershire. The extension to Broadway took the line into the county of Worcestershire (now Hereford & Worcester). Gloucestershire again intrudes for a short distance north of Broadway and to the B4035 road bridge at Weston-sub-Edge, but it is only north of Honeybourne, at Long Marston in fact, that the line actually enters Warwickshire.

The name actually reflects the original intention to reopen the line from Cheltenham Race Course to Stratford-upon-Avon Race Course, but reports at

Visiting royalty: 'King' Class 4-6-0 No 6023 *King Edward II* approaches Gotherington during the 2018 Spring Steam Gala on 28 May 2018. *JW*

the time suggest that such an application for a Light Railway Order (LRO) between those two points was unlikely to succeed due to the length of the line and the inexperience of the applicants in running a railway. In the end, an LRO was granted by the Department of Transport in 1983, which allowed for the reinstatement of the line between Cheltenham Race Course and Broadway. Having successfully raised the capital, the purchase of the 15 miles of trackbed was completed, and later that year the first public train operated (see page 52).

The restoration of the line has been just as incremental as was that of the original line, only instead of just the two years it took the GWR to complete the route, the GWSR, by necessity, took a lot longer. Some 700 yards of relaid track at Toddington enabled the first services to operate in 1984, and by 1985 this had been extended by a further 2,000 yards to Didbrook. Hayles Abbey was reached in 1986, followed by the auspicious return to Winchcombe in 1987, resulting in the arrival of the first steam train for 28 years! By the end of that year track had reached through Greet Tunnel, after which there was a period of consolidation before the next extension to Gretton opened in 1990, Far Stanley four years later in 1994, then Gotherington, some 6½ miles from Toddington, received its first passengers in 1997.

A symbolic laying of track at the site of Cheltenham Race Course station took place in 1998 to promote a share issue, but it was not until 28 December 2000 that GWSR tracks actually reached the station (see page 103). However, a significant amount of engineering work remained on the 3-mile extension, and it was on 17 November 2002 that the first passenger train arrived in the station, to promote an important future relationship with Racing Tours Limited that resulted in the return of race specials to the line. The formal opening was undertaken by HRH The Princess Royal on 7 April 2003, 15 years from the granting of the LRO to the GWSR, and providing the railway with the realisation of the initial part of its dream.

In that time not only had the GWSR reinstated the railway line, but had also worked hard on the infrastructure. It could be said that restoring the infrastructure was a combination of using something old and something new. There was not much to start with, but what there was, such as the station building at Toddington, has been restored to a high standard. Innovation played a significant role, especially at Winchcombe, where the station building and signal box were 'imported' brick by brick from Monmouth Troy and Hall Green respectively. The line was fully signalled, with new signal boxes being installed at Gotherington Loop and Cheltenham Race Course.

During this time financial discipline had been rigorously enforced, with an adopted strict no-borrowing policy in place and using volunteer labour to restore, maintain and operate the railway. The cost was perhaps slower growth, but the positive outcome was that the railway was financially sound and in good shape to meet any 'rainy days'. Little did the GWSR know that there were rainy days ahead and, to continue the metaphor, that the rain would be torrential.

The line had been built on clay, and it could be said that it had been constructed 'on the cheap' by the GWR. The embankments contained significant quantities of ash from local locomotive depots, and the drainage systems were not as efficient as they could, indeed should, have been. Landslips had occurred at Toddington and the location later known as 'Chicken Curve' in the early years of the line, but the GWSR was to be dealt with a series of bitter blows with three landslips in quick succession, two of which, at Gotherington and yet another at 'Chicken Curve', were so serious as to put the railway's very existence into doubt.

The first slippage occurred just north of Cheltenham Race Course station in 2008, resulting in trains having to terminate at Gotherington. Repairs took until February 2009, and cost £300,000. Then in April 2010 a much more serious landslip occurred just south of Gotherington, again closing the line through to Cheltenham Race Course. Newly appointed President Pete Waterman launched a £1 million appeal to cover the cost of repairs, but before they could be completed another calamity hit the railway when, in January 2011, another landslip occurred at 'Chicken Curve'.

The GWSR was facing ruin, but once again the goodwill it had generated over the years came to the rescue: the emergency appeal was extended to cover the 'Chicken Curve' landslip, other heritage lines provided tangible support, and the appeal reached its target. 'Chicken Curve' was repaired, and trains again operated over the full length of the line from October 2012.

During the hiatus of the landslips, there was a little bit of good news, as the line had been extended north from Toddington as far as Stanway Viaduct, and planning permission for the new Broadway station had been approved. Later extensions to Laverton and Little Buckland continued the trend of 'incremental' growth, so typical of the line!

The new Broadway station opened on 30 March 2018, but not before two new share issues, 'The Bridges of Broadway' and 'The Last Mile', had raised a further £1.6 million to complete all the necessary tasks. Year-on-year passenger numbers continue to grow, and the extension to Broadway will only accelerate that growth.

The original 1983 LRO gave permission to reinstate the railway between Cheltenham Race Course and Broadway, but the GWSR actually owns the trackbed beyond Cheltenham Race Course through Hunting Butts Tunnel to a point just north of the Prince of Wales Stadium at Wymans Brook, and there is some local enthusiasm for the GWSR to extend to this point. Beyond, while most of the trackbed is secure and used as a recreational path and cycleway, there are obstacles, particularly where the embankment on which the line ran has been breached for a supermarket development.

Beyond Broadway, the GWSR owns the trackbed for a short distance as for as the Springfield Lane bridge, beyond which the route to Honeybourne is owned by Sustrans and remains free of development. Additionally, as part of the Network Rail (NR) project to reinstate double track on stretches of the Cotswold

HONEYBOURNE: We end where we started, at Honeybourne. On 24 June 1973 preserved ex-Great Western 'Modified Hall' Class No 6998 *Burton Agnes Hall* passes Honeybourne Station South Signal Box hauling the Great Western Society's 'Great Western Returns' Didcot to Hereford charter. On the left is 'Peak' Type 4 No D151, which will later be involved with the charter train as it was required to pilot No 6998 from Worcester back to Didcot on the return journey, as the steam locomotive had sustained a hole in its superheater element causing it to encounter poor steaming issues. *Paul Townsend*

main line, a provision for the return of the GWSR line was made at Honeybourne station. Additionally, local groups outside the GWSR are pushing for the reinstatement of the line from Honeybourne to Stratford-upon-Avon, which presently just serves Long Marston. Such a move could open up the prospect of the GWSR operating through to Stratford, and achieving its original objective. However, there are significant obstacles to be overcome.

Each proposal has its attractions, but how will they benefit the GWSR? A main-line connection would be very beneficial, particularly for race-day specials, but at what financial cost? Would extending south add greatly to passenger numbers, and generate net income? The problem nowadays is that such projects cost significant amounts of money, so great care must be exercised in decided whether any such proposal is viable. After all, the GWSR is a tourist railway, which means that journeys made are for pleasure and therefore subject to the vagaries of the economy.

After the successful extension to Broadway, which has generated significant increased patronage of the line, the official GWSR position is one of consolidation, with attention to infrastructure projects such as a new carriage shed at Winchcombe, and an extension to the David Page Locomotive Works at Toddington. These, and other such projects, will serve to strengthen the railway as well as protecting key assets. The question of whether there should be any further extension will remain, but the answer, for the moment, remains firmly in the future.

Honeybourne

Honeybourne station has had a chequered history since being opened by the Oxford, Worcester & Wolverhampton Railway (OWWR) on 4 June 1853, the day the company extended its line from Evesham to Wolvercot Junction, north of Oxford. Six years later, on 12 July 1859, it became a junction station, when the OWWR opened the branch line to Stratford-upon-Avon. Its importance was enhanced two years later , when in Stratford-upon-Avon the short gap between the OWWR line from Honeybourne and the Stratford upon Avon Railway's branch from Hatton was filled, thus providing a direct link with the Great Western Railway's Paddington to Birmingham main line.

The next major event was the construction of the line to Cheltenham Spa, to which Honeybourne lends its name, with the first section to Broadway opening on 1 August 1904. Also, a cut-off was constructed at this time that provided direct access from Stratford-upon-Avon to the new line to Cheltenham Spa, avoiding the station; this was strategically important to the GWR as it wished to operate fast express services over the route, especially following the subsequent opening of a new direct North Warwickshire Line to Birmingham in 1908. Even though this new connection, from East Loop to West Loop Junctions, provided an effective avoiding line, Honeybourne still remained a significant railway hub.

Goods traffic also contributed to Honeybourne's importance, with yards situated on both sides of the main line; the north yard was located at the Evesham end of the station, and was accessed from the loop line, while the south yard was positioned behind the down platform. Later, a new West Loop Yard was established south of West Loop Junction, which straddled the Cheltenham line.

For the next half-century Honeybourne remained an important junction station, with a host of connection opportunities, but dwindling passenger and freight volumes in the late 1950s were to have a massive impact. The withdrawal of passenger services from the 'Honeybourne Line' in 1960, and to Stratford-upon-Avon in 1965, had a devastating effect on the station's fortunes, but it was the cessation of the local service on the Cotswold Line in 1969 that finally sealed its fate, with closure taking place on 5 May of that year.

However, all was not lost and local developments, both residential and commercial, led to local pressure to reopen the station, which was achieved on 22 May 1981. Initially just a single-platform halt, it was later enlarged following the introduction of double track to the Cotswold Line through Honeybourne in 2011. In addition, there remains the prospect of the GWSR extending north from Broadway at some future date, for which provision was made at the station during the 2011 upgrade.

Honeybourne Junction

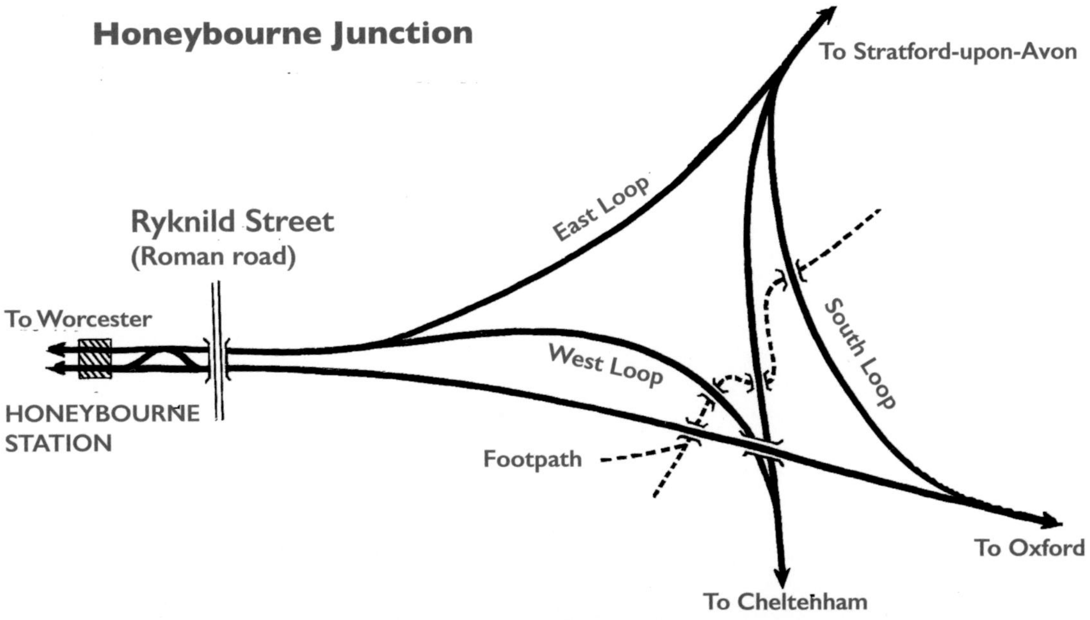

HONEYBOURNE: This remarkable photograph of Honeybourne is thought to have been taken around 1882. It is looking from the up platform towards Oxford and shows the station building on the down side, which survived through to closure, and had replaced the original Brunel 'Chalet'-style building in 1872. Of note is the tall signal box, so built to provide the signalman with a clear view over the Station Road bridge. Station Road is part of Icknield Street, a Roman road that traverses the area. On the right, beyond the station building, is a double-slotted semaphore signal gantry that protects the junction with the Stratford line, beyond the road bridge, while the locomotive is in the process of running round its train prior to working forward to Stratford-upon-Avon. The photograph has been kindly supplied by well-known railway author and photographer Michael Clemens, who thinks it might have a family connection as the name of an aunt of his is inscribed on the original print. Although he never knew this aunt – she died before he was born – an uncle of hers who worked on the line was unfortunately killed while 'larking about' on an engine in 1884. The aunt in question was born in 1884, so would not have known her unfortunate uncle, but as her name is on the original photograph it does pose the question as to whether that uncle is one of the individuals featured. *Michael Clemens collection*

HONEYBOURNE: These three contrasting views of Honeybourne reflect its changing fortunes from a bustling junction to a wayside halt. The first shows the station just prior to closure in 1969, with the 1872 building still intact and seemingly little changed from the 1882 photograph on the previous page. The footbridge remains in situ, although the up platform is now infested with weeds. Station South Signal Box can be seen through the bridge arch, and a lower-quadrant bracket signal stands in the spot once occupied by the original signal box.

Seen from the same vantage point in July 1987, the station has gone through the years of closure, and is again open although the facilities provided do challenge the definition of what is 'basic', as they ooze that stench of dereliction. Still, importantly the station is again open as a Class 101 DMU approaches forming an Oxford-Worcester Shrub Hill all-stations service.

In the 2017 view First Great Western (now Great Western Railway) Class 166 DMU No 166207 approaches while forming a London Paddington-Worcester Shrub Hill service. Ironically, the new station with its mammoth step-free access footbridge has fewer facilities for passengers than in 1981; the latter at least had a basic Portaloo unisex toilet. The new station does have good car parking facilities, though.
R. C. Swift/Geoff Dowling/JW

Further reading:
The Cotswold Line
Past and Present
by John Stretton and Tim Maddocks.

Covering the line from Oxford to Worcester that passes through Honeybourne.

ISBN: 978185895 275 8

Opposite and below: **HONEYBOURNE:** Looking down from the road bridge on 24 April 1982, just under a year after the station reopened, the forlorn remains of what was once a bustling junction station are laid bare. Contrasting with the old down platform, recently relaid upon reopening, the old island platform is now a weed-infested wasteland. In the background are the remains of the goods yard, while the loop lines, which date back to the quadrupling scheme of 1904, are also still in situ on the right, although now only serving the Long Marston depot. On the left the formation of the south goods yard can still clearly be seen. Class 50 No 50037 *Illustrious* passes with an up express. The bracket signal survives, controlled from the now locked-out Station South Signal Box.

From roughly the same viewpoint on 14 October 2017 there is much change to see. A car park occupies the area of the South Yard, while modern, but basic, waiting shelters are provided on each platform. The island platform has been reinstated, accessed by a large step-free footbridge. Note, too, the residential properties that back onto the station, illustrating how the area has been developed in recent years. Approaching is a First Great Western (now Great Western Railway) High Speed Train with Class 43 power car No 43133 leading. *Both JW*

HONEYBOURNE: The full glory that was Honeybourne. This view was recorded on 4 August 1964 and shows a Tyseley-based Class 116 DMU standing in the down main platform, probably forming an all-stations service to Worcester. The canopy of the main station building can be seen on the right just beyond the footbridge that serves all the platforms as well as spanning the four running lines. The island platform also has passenger facilities together with a substantial canopy that covers both platform faces. A smaller, brick-built waiting room occupies the far platform, while a steam locomotive can just be seen through the far left-hand arch of Icknield Road bridge, taking water.

The contrasting scene on 14 October 2017 shows a First Great Western (now Great Western Railway) High Speed Train, with Class 43 power car No 43129 leading, arriving at Honeybourne with a Didcot Parkway-Worcester Foregate Street working. The new island platform, reinstated as part of the 2011 Cotswold Line redoubling project, is on the left, served by the giant walkway of the step-free footbridge. There is one notable survivor from the past, however, as the right-hand spear-top iron fence looks very much like that featured in the 1964 photograph. *Peter Shoesmith/ JW*

Honeybourne
Way Out
First

HONEYBOURNE JUNCTIONS AND STATION SOUTH SIGNAL BOX: This early 1960s view of the complex layout at Honeybourne, governed by the Station South signal box, was taken from the road bridge prior to rationalisation. Note the goods loop and siding behind the signal box, while the tall repeater signal is so positioned as to be seen by drivers of approaching up trains above the parapet of the road bridge. One thing is certain, though – the lamp-man needed a good head for heights!

A similar position in 1976 following rationalisation shows the singled main line nearest to Station South Signal Box. On the left is the spur to the East Loop, which joined the Cheltenham line at East Loop Junction, then continuing to Stratford-upon-Avon. West Loop diverges from East Loop just out of sight beyond the distant curve, and joins the Cheltenham line immediately to the south of the main-line bridge (see the map on page 11). Also in this view is the old North Loop signal box, closed in 1933, now in private hands and positioned by the white house on the right. It is now located in Toddington station car park.

A much simpler formation now exists, as seen on 14 October 2017, as a First Great Western (now Great Western Railway) HST, with Class 43 power car No 43031 leading, approaches Honeybourne station. The connection to Long Marston is to the west of the station, with the line running along what was the old up slow line formation, before reaching a ground frame that controls access to the short branch. *Lens of Sutton/Paul Dorney/JW*

HONEYBOURNE STRATFORD PLATFORM: This is Honeybourne in the 1930s, with a '1400' Class tank locomotive sitting in the dedicated Stratford-upon-Avon branch platform awaiting departure. The locomotive stands next to the water crane and will likely have had its tanks replenished, while the driver looks to be engaged in the task of applying oil to key parts of his steed. Note the 'Honeybourne Junction' running-in board, which details the onward travel options from the station, and the enamel 'Dewars Whisky' advertisement.

Four years after closure of the station, the scene from the road bridge shows considerable change. Both the island and Stratford branch platforms are bereft of all buildings and being reclaimed by nature. An engineer's train, headed by 'Peak' Type 4 No 151 (later Class 46 No 46014), draws out of the remains of the up-side goods yard on 24 June 1973. The now singled main line can be seen on the extreme left.

There is the semblance of a double-track formation running along the course of the old slow lines, with that on the right being the access line to the Long Marston branch, which serves a former Ministry of Defence establishment, now privately owned and dealing with railway maintenance and stock storage. Making its way to Long Marston is a Pathfinder Tours enthusiasts' special on 1 April 2017, headed by Direct Rail Services Class 37/7 No 37716. Of interest is the truncated track sitting alongside what was once the down slow platform, which has been kept clear for the future potential use of the GWSR, should it decide to extend north from Broadway. *Lens of Sutton/Paul Townsend/JW*

HONEYBOURNE: The date is 5 March 1960, and 0-6-0 pannier tank No 8488 rolls into Honeybourne at the head of just one coach, about to form the 9.45am service to Cheltenham St James. This is the last day of the passenger service on the Honeybourne Line, which resulted in all the intermediate stations closing. On a practical note, the large running-in board will need attention due to the lost connections caused by the withdrawal of the passenger service. In the background '2251' Class 0-6-0 No 2273 awaits its next duty.

The new step-free footbridge, a product of the station's regeneration as part of the Cotswold Line redoubling, is now the dominant feature as it swoops over the main line, then descends gently onto the new platform. It has a landing some way down, off which is a spur that would be very useful should the GWSR decide to extend its line, which importantly would provide the heritage line with a main-line connection. Approaching is First Great Western Class 166 'Turbo' DMU No 166203 forming a service for London Paddington on 1 April 2017. *John Stretton/JW*

HONEYBOURNE WEST LOOP JUNCTION: The West Loop connected Honeybourne station with the through Stratford-upon-Avon to Cheltenham line, the actual junction being situated on the south side of the rail bridge that carries the Cotswold main line over the formation. Honeybourne West Loop Signal Box stood in the 'V' of the junction, on the Stratford side of the main-line bridge. When West Loop Yard opened in 1960 it was superseded by a new signal box located just within the northern end of the new yard. In February 1964 a down freight off the Stratford-upon-Avon line, consisting of mineral wagons, is seen accelerating away from West Loop Junction in the hands of 'Modified Hall' No 6980 *Llanrumney Hall*.

The scene today from the Mickleton Road bridge shows that the formation has been reclaimed by nature, although the course of the line is clearly defined. Note that the main-line bridge has been replaced by a modern concrete structure, most probably when it was redoubled in 2012. *Tony Bowles/ JW*

HONEYBOURNE WEST LOOP SIDINGS: In 1960 a new goods yard opened to the south of Honeybourne West Loop Junction, primarily to accommodate rerouted iron ore traffic from Banbury following the installation of a new south-facing chord at Racecourse Junction, Stratford-upon-Avon. It contained eight sidings, four on each side of the line to Cheltenham, controlled by a new flat-roofed signal box that opened on 24 April 1960, the same day that the old West Loop Junction signal box closed. The new yard had a short life, closing on 31 January 1966 due to the downturn in iron ore traffic. Later, in 1970, it did enjoy a short period of activity when the down-side yard reopened to allow goods trains destined for Long Marston to run round following the closure of the north-to-east curve. However, closure of the yard for good came about in 1981 with the reinstatement of the north-to-east curve. The 'new' signal box had been decommissioned in 1980 and subsequently demolished. In the first of these three pictures reflecting the life of the yard, a northbound freight is working through the yard in April 1964 hauled by 'Grange' No 6831 *Bearley Grange*, while on the left, positioned behind the signal box, another freight awaits departure.

The scene a few years later from the Mickleton Road bridge, following the reinstatement of the north-to-east chord, shows the signal box closed and the main line being lifted. In the foreground is the bracket signal that protected the junction; the right-hand arm (as you look at the picture) was for Honeybourne station, and the left-hand arm for straight on to Stratford-upon-Avon.

In the view southwards today from the Mickleton Road bridge the area had been reclaimed by nature, but the course of the railway is still identifiable. Maybe the most distinctive feature are the cables running along the top of the picture, which look to be the very same as those seen in the photograph above. *J. R. Newman, Colour Rail/Tony Bowles/JW*

Weston-sub-Edge and Broadway

WESTON-SUB-EDGE: Originally named 'Bretforton and Weston-sub-Edge' when it opened on 1 August 1904, the station was 2 miles and 18 chains from Honeybourne East Loop. The name of this out-of-the-way station was mercifully shortened to just 'Weston-sub-Edge' as of 1 May 1907, and was the first station south from Honeybourne on the new line. It had a small goods yard positioned at the north end of the station on the down (southbound) side, which was controlled by the adjacent signal box positioned on the up (northbound) side. Goods facilities were withdrawn on 25 September 1950, and the signal box closed a couple of weeks later. The station itself closed on 7 March 1960 and nothing remains of the site except for the station master's house, now in private hands. However, a notable survivor is the waiting room on the up platform, which avoided demolition, and has since been dismantled and re-erected on Platform 2 of the Llangollen Railway's Carrog station.

This early view of the station, looking north, was no doubt taken soon after opening. A railmotor stands in the up platform forming a service for Honeybourne. The main station building is opposite, on the down side, while behind it is the goods yard where a goods van can be seen. What appears to be a shunting locomotive is operating near the main line connection, opposite to which is the signal box. This view is taken from what is now the B4035 road bridge.
Archive Images

WESTON-SUB-EDGE: The first view, also taken from the road bridge, dates from just before the outbreak of the Second World War. There has been little change since opening, and the station has that 'well looked after' appearance. The up platform waiting room, which now stands at Carrog, can be seen tucked away between the trees opposite the main station building.

Following closure, the trackbed through the station site remains clear in this March 2018 view, again taken from the B4035 road bridge. The building on the far right is the old station master's house.

At Carrog the waiting room provides shelter for the Llangollen Railway's passengers. Carrog is the current terminus of the line, which will shortly be extended through to Corwen. Showing a typical branch-line station scene with milk churns and a trunk, the former Weston-sub-Edge building certainly adds to the atmosphere, which is further enhanced by the presence of GWR 'Dukedog' '3200' Class 4-4-0 No 9017 on 23 March 2009. The unusual 'Dukedog' name derives from when the class were rebuilt by the GWR in 1936 using boilers from the 'Duke' Class and frames from the 'Bulldog' Class. *Lens of Sutton, JW (2)*

WILLERSEY HALT: The site of Willersey Halt, perched on an embankment on the south side of Badsey Lane, is now totally overgrown to the extent that a present-day shot would be pointless. Better to remember it as it was, as illustrated in this charming September 1928 scene, highlighted by a schoolboy of the day, complete with cap, jacket and regulation short trousers, waiting on the up platform possibly for the train to take him to school. The halt, 3 miles and 47 chains from Honeybourne East Loop, served the nearby village of the same name and was located roughly midway between Weston-sub-Edge and Broadway stations. Consisting of a couple of 100-foot wooden platforms (later extended to 152 feet), it opened in or around October 1904 – the exact date is unclear. As with the other halts on the line, each platform was provided with a GWR-pattern 'Pagoda' corrugated-iron shelter, one of which has been rescued by Bryan Nicholls and is now at Gotherington West (see page 87). Access was by means of a walkway from the road below. It closed on 7 March 1960, and all trace has been swept away and the site reclaimed by nature. Close inspection reveals a bridge in the distance, which carries the Willersey to Broadway road. *Clarence Gilbert/Roger Carpenter Collection*

WILLERSEY HALT: Although little under a year from closure, Willersey Halt still looks pristine in this view taken on 19 July 1959. The schoolboy in the earlier scene was standing in front of the sign positioned at the end of the up platform (on the left in this scene). The parapets of the Badsey Lane bridge can be seen beyond the platforms. *H. C. Casserley*

BROADWAY station opened on 1 August 1904; it is situated 4 miles and 73 chains from Honeybourne East Loop, and around three-quarters of a mile from Broadway village, nowadays a well-known tourist attraction, on the main road to Evesham. Goods facilities were provided, with the yard and shed being positioned to the south of the station. The signal box was positioned immediately to the south of the main road bridge, and was thus located centrally between the station and goods yard. The station closed to passengers on 7 March 1960, and the signal box on 10 October of that year, while the goods yard survived until 1 June 1964. This fascinating scene looking north shows the new Broadway station, so new in fact that the workmen have still to complete the up platform surface. Given also that the background trees are still in leaf, this scene must date to around the time of opening. The passengers on the down platform all appear to be prosperous, judging by their dress, reflecting the local affluence. Indeed, given that this has all the hallmarks of a professionally produced photograph, there is a hint that it may even have been 'staged', given the attitude of the people. That said, it still provides a superb illustration of the new station, looking north towards Honeybourne. One thing of note is that 'Gentlemen' seem to have preference, as both platforms provide them with toilet facilities, whereas the 'Ladies' have to make do with their 'Waiting Room' on the down platform. *The Restoration & Archiving Trust*

BROADWAY: During its lifetime the station seems to have changed little, as this late-1950s view reflects. Even the original signage remains, which again reconfirms the two-to-one bias of toilet facilities in favour of the gentlemen. A conversation between two crew members certainly seems to be of substance, judging by their facial interaction, all of which is observed by the schoolboy, still in uniform, either waiting to join the train or possibly expanding his knowledge of local railway operations. Auto-trains formed the basis of passenger services in the latter days, as seen here with GWR '1400' Class 0-4-2T No 1424 at the rear of a two-coach push-pull working bound for Honeybourne.

The new Broadway station is seen here from the incomplete up platform on 8 March 2018, as 'Modified Hall' No 7903 *Foremarke Hall* departs southwards following clearance trials for both locomotive and coaching stock. This view is taken from a point further along the platform than that above and shows the new signal box; the original was positioned next to the down line on the Toddington side of the road bridge. The main span of the former Henley-in-Arden footbridge is in position, but the steps have still to be fitted. *Lens of Sutton/Jack Boskett*

BROADWAY: This 1950s view shows a northbound freight passing through hauled by '4300' Class 2-6-0 No 6324. Note Broadway signal box on the left, perched on top of the embankment just beyond the girders of the road bridge. It closed on 10 October 1960, some months after the withdrawal of the passenger service.

Following closure the station was soon demolished, leaving just a scar on the landscape. The second view was taken on 19 March 1965 from the upper end of Station Drive, with the remnant of the down platform now fenced. '5700' Class 0-6-0PT No 4616 hurries north with a lengthy rake of short-wheelbase mineral wagons forming the 8.20am Cheltenham to Honeybourne pick-up freight. Goods facilities at Broadway had ceased the previous year, on 1 June 1964.

In the present-day scene we are looking south from a position just under the new station's canopy. On the left is Station Drive and a traditional red telephone box, while the new signal box is situated on the opposite up platform, which is in the course of being commissioned. Entering the platform is visiting diesel-hydraulic 'Warship' No D832 *Onslaught* on 28 July 2018. *The Restoration & Archiving Trust, GWR Collection/The Restoration & Archival Trust, John Dagley Morris collection/JW*

BROADWAY is seen in the first view at its lowest point; the date is 14 October 1979, some three years after closure, and the track is in the process of being ripped up. The up line is now reduced to sleepers and chairs, while the down line appears to have been severed just beyond the road bridge. No trace of the station remains, except maybe for the distinctive pine trees. Note the road bridge in the background, and the surviving milepost on the far left.

The new view of Broadway, taken from the opposite side of the running line but pinpointed by the milepost, shows English Electric Type 3, later known as Class 37, No D6948 powering away from the new station with a train for Toddington on 22 March 2018. The new platform-based signal box is on the left, and the reconditioned footbridge, previously at Henley-in-Arden, in the background. Both the signal box and footbridge have yet to be commissioned. Note that the run-round loop is positioned on the old up formation, with the main running line following the course of the old down line. *Martin Loader/JW*

BROADWAY GOODS SHED AND YARD are under construction early in 1904. The shed was situated next to the down line, and careful examination of this scene reveals the station and footbridge situated behind the person who appears to be watching the photographer. A down loop was provided, alongside which was positioned a through road providing direct access to the goods shed. A further three sidings were provided behind the shed, all on a falling gradient of 1 in 50 towards the main road. Rail access to the yard was at a point south of the station, close to the Childswickham Road bridge; it was controlled by a ground frame, release for which came from Broadway signal box. The goods yard closed on 1 June 1964.

Following closure of the goods yard, the goods shed miraculously survived and passed ultimately into GWSR ownership. This 1978 view shows the building vandalised but still in good shape and is viewed from the site of Broadway station, looking south. Note that both running lines remain in situ.

In 2011 the GWSR sold the goods shed to the Caravan Club in order to raise funds to cover the costs of the 'Chicken Curve' landslip and the related loss of operating income. It was a difficult decision, but the railway needed funds urgently. In addition to providing amenities to the caravan site visitors, the Caravan Club also uses the goods shed to store 'The Wanderer', the first horse-drawn caravan built for Dr William Gordon Stables in 1884. Dr Stables travelled thousands of miles in the vehicle, drawn by two horses, as his ambition was to live the life of a 'Gentleman Gypsy'. On 30 March 2018 there was more horsepower on display, as 'Manor' 4-6-0 No 7820 *Dinmore Manor* passes the goods shed as it arrives at Broadway with a train from Cheltenham Race Course. *The Restoration & Archiving Trust/Martin Loader/JW*

BROADWAY GOODS YARD: This is the view looking north towards the site of the station, with the goods shed on the right, with its extended platform and a corrugated-iron extension with two access points. By this time the entire structure was derelict, although still looking in a reasonable condition. Note that the up line has now been lifted, with just the sleepers and chairs in situ – but not for long.

A closer view of the revamped goods shed is provided on 22 March 2018, as Southern Railway 'Merchant Navy' No 35006 *Peninsular & Oriental S.N. Co* storms away from Broadway station.

The layout of the entrance to the goods yard is still evident by the shape of the land adjoining the railway, now in the hands of the Caravan Club. The space is used by touring caravans and mobile homes, while the main entrance to the old goods shed in now totally glazed. *Martin Loader/JW (2)*

South from Broadway

SOUTH FROM BROADWAY Gentle but adverse gradients dictate the passage into Broadway from each direction, with the station standing on the summit. For around 2 miles south of the station the railway runs along a low embankment to the site of Laverton Halt. This section affords fine views of both the Cotswold Hills to the east and a panorama to the west across the Vale of Evesham towards the River Severn and the Malvern Hills.

Groundwork in connection with the extension to Broadway confirmed that it shared characteristics with the line to the south, including blocked culverts and drains, which could result in future instability. A programme of remedial work was put in place, together with the 'Bridges for Broadway' appeal to fund necessary, and in some instances extensive, repairs to structures at Broadway itself, as well as those at Childswickham Road, Pry Lane, Peasebrook Farm and Little Buckland.

This is the view looking over the Vale of Evesham with No 7820 *Dinmore Manor* heading a southbound service on 28 October 2018. The train, having just departed from Broadway, is working along the embankment between the Childswickham and Pry Lane bridges. *JW*

THE VALE OF EVESHAM is seen from the Winchcombe Way footpath, with the picturesque village of Laverton, built in traditional Cotswold stone, in the foreground and Dumbleton Hill providing the backdrop. With the extension of GWSR services to Broadway, this will become one of the defining views of the railway. On a glorious autumnal morning in October 2017, the GWSR's Class 117 diesel multiple unit (DMU) is seen making its way to the railway's temporary northern terminus at Buckland. *JW*

LITTLE BUCKLAND BRIDGE: These two views of the reconstructed Little Buckland bridge were taken on 14 October 2017 It is one of the structures included in the 'Bridges for Broadway' appeal that funded the necessary rebuilding work on the structures located between Stanton Cutting and Broadway. In the first, Class 117 Driving Motor Brake Second (DMBS) No W51363 leads a DMU formation as it crosses the bridge, which spans the road to Aston Somerville. The new brickwork on the wing wall and abutment is clearly evident. Note, too, that care needs to be taken during particularly wet weather, as the flooding depth measurement is up to 9 feet of water – enough to sink a car without trace!

Looking across the deck of the bridge, Class 117 DMBS car No 51360 is the lead vehicle of a three-car DMU heading for the new stop board at Buckland. This view shows the refurbished ironwork and rebuilt abutments to good effect. *Both JW*

LAVERTON HALT, 7 miles and 3 chains from Honeybourne East Loop opened on 14 August 1905 and was positioned on the Toddington side of a bridge under which passed the road from Laverton to Wormington. The original wooden platforms were 100 feet in length, later extended to 158 feet. Each platform was provided with the traditional GWR 'Pagoda' corrugated waiting shelter. The halt closed on 7 March 1960. There is a 'double take' here on 19 July 1959, as both pictures record the arrival of '4500' Class 'Prairie' 2-6-2T No 5514, heading the 2.15pm Saturdays-only Broadway-Cheltenham St James service. The photographs were taken by well-known father and son railway photographers H. C. Casserley (top) and R. M. Casserley (centre), and offer excellent views of the halt. Note Casserley senior positioned at the end of the platform in his son's photograph. The girder supporting the bridge over the roadway can be seen between the running lines beneath the last coach of the train.

Looking towards Broadway on 28 May 2018, the third picture shows No 35006 *Peninsular & Oriental S.N. Co* approaching with a service for Cheltenham Race Course. By necessity, this view is taken from a point roughly halfway along where the down platform stood; note the position of the footpath leading to the roadway on the right. The road bridge is new, having been removed a few years ago to allow large vehicles access to the nearby gas pipeline pumping station, and subsequently replaced by TRANSCO, which operates the pipeline. *H. C. Casserley/R. M. Casserley/JW*

STANTON CUTTING: A northbound permanent way train attending to the route's telegraph poles works north through Stanton Cutting and approaches the then A46 road bridge on 1 March 1964, hauled by GWR 'Grange' No 6846 *Ruckley Grange*. Note the car parked alongside the road, which looks like a Ford Anglia, no doubt belonging to photographer Michael Mensing. Just visible in the murky background is an aqueduct that doubles as a footbridge.

Nowadays the A46 has become the B4632, the former main road having been diverted and upgraded. The bridge remains, however, and at some point the retaining wall has been partially clad with an coat of protecting material. The formation remains the same, except for the loss of what was the up line, as the GWSR use the original down formation for its line. On 29 December 2017 the remains of a heavy snowfall a few days earlier greet No D6948 on a working from Cheltenham Race Course through to the temporary stop board at Buckland, then the northern limit of the line. *Michael Mensing, JW collection/JW*

STANTON CUTTING: That innocuous-looking footbridge has a history! First, it is more than just a footbridge, as it doubles as an aqueduct carrying a local stream across the railway, with a trough positioned beneath the walkway. Second, on 11 December 1941 it was the focus of the Luftwaffe, whether intentionally or not, when together with Weston-sub-Edge it was bombed. Damage at the latter was minimal, but at Stanton Cutting the down line received a direct hit, causing it to be lifted 8 feet into the air and creating a huge crater together with collateral damage to the up line. Shrapnel damaged the railings of the aqueduct, the distortion of which remains to be seen today. The route at that time was of strategic importance, and the up line was reopened on 14 December, with the down line returning to service the following day after the infilling of the huge bomb crater.

Passing beneath the aqueduct on 28 May 2018 is BR Standard 'Britannia' 'Pacific' No 70013 *Oliver Cromwell* at the head of a service from Broadway to Cheltenham Race Course. Note the bent railing on the second panel to the left of the train. *Both JW*

STANWAY VIADUCT: Just north of Toddington station stands Stanway Viaduct, the most significant engineering structure on the line. Completed in 1904, this impressive 15-arch bridge is 210 yards long and 50 feet tall at its highest point. It again has some history attached as the No 10 arch collapsed at 8.15am on 13 November 1903, bringing down with it a 14-ton steam crane. Its driver survived the impact and was placed under No 9 arch to recover, but this, too, unfortunately also caved in, burying and inflicting further injury on the unfortunate driver. Then, while he was being dug out, No 8 arch also collapsed. The driver did not recover from his injuries, but other workers had miraculous escapes during the catastrophe. The cause was never established, but was likely to be a combination of recent poor weather, ground conditions, premature withdrawal of the timber supports, the weight of the crane and the type of mortar used. Needless to say, following reconstruction of the collapsed arches, the viaduct has since proven itself fit for purpose. The first picture shows the aftermath of the collapse. A locomotive can be seen on the far left on a works train, but note also how precariously the track seems to be suspended over a gully.

Stanway Viaduct, in all its glory, is seen through the trees from the B4632 road on a damp 30 March 2018, with GWR '2800' Class 2-8-0 No 2807 heading north with a train for Broadway. A member of the footplate crew can be seen surveying the scene from the viaduct as he straddles the gap between footplate and tender. The arches that collapsed are those on the right. *Archive Images/JW*

STANWAY VIADUCT: On 13 June 2004 the viaduct is bereft of track but there are plenty of participants in a sponsored walk aimed at once again seeing trains work across this magnificent structure. The walk covered the trackbed of the line from just north of Toddington to Broadway and raised valuable funds towards the southern extension to Cheltenham Race Course. This is the scene looking south across the viaduct and a handful of the reported 191 participants enjoying both the weather and the exercise.

The viaduct reopened to trains in May 2010, followed by incremental extensions to Laverton in 2011, Buckland in 2017 and finally Broadway in 2018. The prospect of seeing a pair of unrebuilt Bulleid 'Pacifics' storming across the viaduct at the future date was probably beyond the wildest dreams of those walkers back in 2004, but on 30 May 2015 it happened: two visiting 'Spam Cans', the wartime nickname for these locomotives, are seen double-heading on the approach to the viaduct, with 'West Country' No 34092 *City of Wells* leading classmate No 34007 *Wadebridge*. *Steve Widdowson/JW*

STANWAY VIADUCT: This distant view of Stanway Viaduct illustrates how well it blends into the landscape. Heading across the viaduct on 10 June 2018 is No 7820 *Dinmore Manor* working a Cheltenham Race Course to Broadway service. *JW*

Toddington

Toddington station opened on 1 December 1904, and was some 9 miles and 36 chains from Honeybourne East Loop. The station is placed between the villages of Toddington and Stanway, the former around a mile distant to the west, the latter around half a mile to the east. The former lent its name to the station, the latter to the nearby viaduct.

The main station building is on the up side, with just a waiting shelter provided on the opposite platform, and both remain in situ today. However, Toddington's importance was not as a passenger station, but for its goods facilities, which handled a wide range of products. A large goods yard was provided to the south of the station that boasted both a goods shed and a packing shed, the latter reflecting Toddington's location as a central point of dispatch for the produce of the local fruit growers, the major employers in the area. The goods yard also proved useful as a stabling point for the many race-day specials that served meetings at Cheltenham.

There were few changes over the ensuing decades, although traffic and receipts were declining, but the Second World War provided a temporary reverse in the station's fortunes. However, the post-war era saw further decline, particularly due to the continued fall in goods traffic, which was being lost to the emerging road haulage industry.

Toddington station closed, together with all its neighbours along the line, on 7 March 1960, but the goods yard was to survive for a few years more, not closing until 3 January 1967. Miraculously, the buildings on both platforms survived, although not the platforms themselves. Other notable survivors were the goods shed and signal box.

From a desolate wasteland after total closure in 1976, and track-lifting a few years later, salvation came in 1981 when the site was leased to the Gloucestershire Warwickshire Railway Trust, and Toddington became its headquarters.

TODDINGTON: This unusual viewpoint of Toddington station was taken under the strictest of supervision during a photographers' charter, with No 4270 approaching very slowly with a rake of freight vans and wagons in tow. It does also provide an excellent view of the station, ranging from the period lamp posts to the replacement water tower. Note the steelwork that supports the station's canopy. *JW*

TODDINGTON: Looking north towards Broadway in 1952 from what is now the B4077 road bridge, Toddington's Down Inner Home signal dominates the scene. Note how the embankment beside the distant curve seems to bulge a little – this was the site of an early landslip that has been buttressed by a retaining wall.

The station is accessed by a driveway off the B4077, and the bridge that carries this road over the line is positioned at the north end of the platforms. It affords good views of the line in each direction, and this view was taken from the east side of the bridge on 25 July 1964, looking north into the cutting, as GWR 'Hall' 4-6-0 No 4908 *Broome Hall* approaches the closed station with a southbound Summer Saturday holiday working.

In 1964 the line was double track throughout, but the GWSR operates as a single line with station loops to allow trains to cross. On 28 October 2015 Southern Region electro-diesel No E6036 (later Class 73 No 73129) works along Toddington's down loop with just one empty bolster wagon in tow, while engaged on engineering duties. Note the extent of the station loop beyond the protecting signals. The main line curves to the right in the distance towards Stanway Viaduct, alongside which is a long siding used for the stabling of passenger stock, and the retaining wall that supports the embankment. *Roger Carpenter, P. J. Garland collection/Tony Bowles/JW*

TODDINGTON: This panoramic view was taken looking south from the footbridge in 1952, showing the extent of the goods yard. The goods shed is on the left with the entrance to the dock closed off, while to the right is the packing shed, which has a rake of wagons berthed alongside. Note the sizeable ventilation louvres on its roof, as the fruit passing through the shed was likely to be a bit aromatic. A couple of grounded van bodies can be seen next to the vacant dock, which was known as 'The Parlour'. A bicycle is propped up against the station building wall, its owner possibly using the facilities just around the corner.

A fascinating scene is provided by the second picture, looking from the B4077 road bridge towards the station as begrimed GWR '4500' Class 'Prairie' 2-6-2T No 5542 is in the process of setting back into the yard with the 8.20am Cheltenham Spa (St James)-Evesham pick-up freight on 31 August 1964. Note that the station buildings remain intact, but the platforms and footbridge have been removed. The signal box is just visible on the far left, while to the right is the goods shed, and further to the right, partly obscured by the chimneys of the station building, the packing shed. It is good to note that No 5542 survived, and is based on the GWSR today.

In late June 1981 there is still desolation – and hope. The track had been lifted two years earlier, but now the Gloucestershire Warwickshire Railway Trust has secured the lease of the station area and has already relaid a couple of track panels between the signal box and goods shed. Standing on the new trackwork are the first arrivals; on the right is GWR '2800' Class 2-8-0 No 2807 and 'Manor' No 7821 *Ditcheat Manor*, while on the left is No 2807's tender and Hudswell Clark 0-6-0 diesel-mechanical shunter No D615. The station buildings have survived, and look in reasonable shape, although the main building seems to have lost one of it chimneys. However, the absence of track through the station is matched also by the lack of platforms, which had been removed even before the line closed. *Roger Carpenter, P. J. Garland collection/The Restoration & Archiving Trust, John Dagley Morris collection/The Restoration & Archiving Trust, Tony Bowles*

TODDINGTON: This was the view from the footbridge on 27 August 2008, as BR Class 9F 2-10-0 No 92203 *Black Prince* enters Toddington's up platform with a service from Cheltenham Race Course. A fine array of motive power is on display, with examples from both the steam and diesel fleets present. However, this view also shows the original goods shed to good effect, now being used as a machine shop, while to the right is the large David Page Building, which is the new locomotive depot and workshops. The goods yard, out of the picture to the right, now provides ample car parking space for visitors. *JW*

TODDINGTON: The scene today reflects the progress that the GWSR has made over the years. Toddington is now the headquarters of the heritage line with a busy throughput of passengers, some tens of thousands more than in the days of the GWR and BR. Drawing into Platform 2 on 14 October 2017 is English Electric Type 1 No D8137 (later Class 20 No 20137) at the head of a terminating service from Cheltenham Race Course, while the DMU, with DMBS No W51360 leading, awaits departure as a shuttle service to Buckland, then the northern terminus of the line pending reopening to Broadway. Note that the footbridge, which is a more recent addition to the station, is a near copy of the original, which was removed when the station closed. *JW*

TODDINGTON station has been closed for more than two years as GWR 'Hall' 4-6-0 No 6984 *Owsden Hall* passes through with a Bristol-bound freight that has originated at Crewe. The date is 29 August 1962, and the main station building looks to be in reasonable shape. Note that while the platforms remain, the footbridge has been removed. A water crane remains positioned at the end of the down platform, fed from the large water tank that can be seen behind the tender of the 'Hall'.

The second view is full of interest, especially when compared with the earlier scene. It is the summer of 1971, and the platforms have now been removed, except for a last remnant of the down platform and ramp, which sits forlornly awaiting its demise. Note too that the water crane has gone, and very likely also the large elevated water tank, whose fate cannot be confirmed at this point as its location is hidden behind the trees that border the down side. The buildings on both sides of the line remain in reasonable condition, and note too the old station master's house on the left. The track leading to the goods yard diverges to the left, while the facing brick wall beyond denotes the location of the bay platform, known as 'The Parlour'; this was used to stable stock as well as being the loading point for the 17-gallon milk churns used by the numerous local dairy farms that sent their produce away by rail. *The Restoration & Archiving Trust, Tony Bowles/The Restoration & Archiving Trust, GWR collection*

TODDINGTON: Moving forward 20 years, the station is now firmly back in business, and even has a GWR 'Castle' to recall the glory days of 'The Cornishman' express. It is August 1991, and Tyseley-based No 5080 *Defiant* is visiting the GWSR for a period, and stands at the head of a working to Winchcombe and the then southern terminus at Gretton, where a run-round loop was located. A GWR 'Prairie' tank has been stabled in the reinstated 'Parlour' siding. Reinstatement of the footbridge is still to take place, with access to the down platform by means of the foot crossing presently straddled by *Defiant*'s leading pony truck.

The foot crossing remains in public use today, albeit moved a short distance further from the platform ramps. Looking back from the station car park on 29 October 2016 we see 'The Parlour' bay platform occupied by electro-diesel No E6036, while the station is occupied by the Class 117 DMU, which will soon head north towards Laverton, and an impatient No 7820 *Dinmore Manor*, which seems keen to get its 'Spooky Special' to Cheltenham Race Course on the move. The now reinstated footbridge can be seen above the DMU. *Both JW*

TODDINGTON is seen again on a crisp November day in 1967, but with evidence of recent heavy rain judging by the size of the puddle that conveniently provides a reflection of passing Gloucester Railway Carriage & Wagon-built single-car unit No M55004; these vehicles were later affectionately known as 'Bubble Cars'. The train is a morning service from Leamington Spa to Gloucester Central. Although now seven years after closure, the station building seems to remain in a reasonable state of repair.

Although No M55004 later succumbed to the cutter's torch, a number of GRC&W-built single-car units (later designated Class 122) were saved. Indeed one, coincidentally No W55003, which also saw service on the Honeybourne Line for British Railways, is seen standing in the now fully restored Toddington station on 7 July 2012. The station area is quiet for a summer Saturday, entirely due to the reduced service operating at the time between Hayles Abbey and Laverton due to the serious landslip at 'Chicken Curve' near Winchcombe. *The Restoration & Archiving Trust, John Dagley Morris collection /JW*

TODDINGTON: Unfortunately little is known about the train and date of this image, taken from the south end of Toddington station, save that it is of a southbound Class 47-hauled coal train taken some time in the early 1970s. However, there is quite a lot of detail to note, starting with the position of all the signals, which indicates that the signal box is switched out – by this time the signalling block section probably extended from Cheltenham Lansdown Road to Long Marston. Note that the goods loop with catch point has by now been severed, and a sleeper chained to the stub can just be seen beyond the goods shed. The shed itself survives and, judging by the part of the sign visible, remains in use; the rail access portal seems to have been bricked up, though.

Today's view was taken from a little closer to the station, and thus provides a good impression of the size of the goods yard at Toddington, now a spacious car park that is particularly useful for Cheltenham race-day specials. The signal box is manned on this occasion, as all the signals are at danger as the departure of No 7903 *Foremarke Hall* is still some minutes away. A GWR parcels coach occupies the siding on the right, previously known as 'The Parlour', while the old goods shed has been restored with the portal reopened, although it is now used as a machine shop. To the right is the newer David Page Locomotive Workshops. A member of the footplate team looks to be in deep conversation with his colleague, all of which is observed by a family, whose young son will hopefully grow up wanting to be an engine driver! *The Restoration & Archiving Trust, Mike Shorland collection/JW*

TODDINGTON: Desolation: vandalised and virtually abandoned, the inside of Toddington signal box looks a sorry sight in December 1979, three years after the passing of the last train. The box had opened in December 1904 when the line was extended from Broadway and, as well as being an important intermediate box on the line, it also was responsible for the adjacent goods yard. This view reflects the neglect since 1976, with what looks like the ingress of a climbing plant coiling itself around the frame and levers, and the block instruments have been ripped out. The signalman's chair has been left strewn over the floor and the windows smashed. However, what was most important was that the building had not been torched or demolished, although just prior to ownership passing to the GWSR the frame was removed and sold to the Gwili Railway. *The Restoration & Archiving Trust, Tony Bowles*

TODDINGTON: Restoration: this is the immaculate interior of Toddington signal box today, as the signalman is in the process of 'setting the road' for a train to Winchcombe. Above him is the track diagram for the area he controls, annotated with the location of all the signals and points in his section, with the shelf below carrying all the block instruments. Note the row of brass electric locking release plungers above each lever, which the signalman is required to depress in certain circumstances to unlock the lever, which can then be pulled over. Each lever is colour-coded: red for a stop signal, red with a white band for an advanced starter signal, black for mechanical points, blue for a mechanical facing point lock, and blue and black for a combined points and facing point lock, while the red and black striped lever is for switching out the signal box when unmanned. Note that three levers are shorter than the rest, which denotes that they control an electrically operated signal or set of points. Having lost the original frame to the Gwili Railway, the frame now in situ came to the GWSR from the North Warwickshire Line signal box at Earlswood. *JW*

TODDINGTON: In 1984, early days for the embryo GWSR, trains operated from Toddington along a straight length of track laid alongside the old goods yard. Within 12 months, though, the line had been extended as far as Didbrook. Traction during this period was provided by Avonside 0-4-0T *Cadbury No 1*, which is seen passing Toddington signal box on a pleasant summer day in 1984. The locomotive, Works No 1977 of 1925, is a product of the Bristol-based Avonside Engine Company, which traded between 1864 and 1934, and the loco spent all its working life on the Bourneville Works Railway within the Cadbury factory complex. When that system closed in 1976 it was donated to the Birmingham Railway Museum, then a long-term loan was agreed with the GWSR and it is famous for hauling the first revenue-earning train on the heritage line. It is now back at Tyseley, cosmetically restored, but awaiting a full overhaul.

It is interesting to note how at first glance little has changed over the intervening 30 years between these two images. GWR 'Manor' 4-6-0 No 7820 *Dinmore Manor* passes the now operational Toddington signal box in April 2014, with its attendant array of semaphore signals. It is in the background where the significant changes can be seen, namely the new footbridge and reinstated Platform 2. *The Restoration & Archiving Trust, Tony Bowles/JW*

TODDINGTON: This more distant view is looking back towards Toddington station and signal box, and at the latter an important part of railway operation is about to take place with the signalman offering the single-line 'token' for the next section to the driver of No 4270. The train has just departed from Toddington station on 11 September 2016, and is seen winding over the pointwork from what was the up platform in BR days on the approach to the signal box. Note how the use of a long telephoto lens accentuates the dipped rail joints.

Toddington yard is seen on 11 September 2016, with an array of motive power on show, including two shunting locomotives with interesting backgrounds. On the far left is the Yorkshire Engine Company's 0-6-0 No 372 *Des*, Works No 2760 of 1959, built initially for the Port of London Authority prior to moving to Allied Steel & Wire at Cardiff in 1971. It moved to Toddington in 1999. Alongside is a Drewry 0-6-0 shunter , which has been restored to look like a BR Class 04 locomotive and carries the fictitious number of 11230. It was never a BR machine, being one of a pair that spent most of their working lives at Willington Power Station, near Derby, arriving at Toddington in 2003. Stabled on depot road No 9, with scaffolding surrounding it cab, is Class 117 DMBS No W51360. Standing beneath the portable crane is No E6036 (later BR Class 73/1 No 73129), behind which is Class 20 No. 20035; this is an interesting locomotive as it still carries the livery of French operator Compagnie de Chemins des Fer Départementaux (CFD), for whom it worked for several years prior to be repatriated; it is based at Toddington for component recovery to keep No D8137 active. On the right is 'Peak' Class 45/1 No 45149 (formerly D135), one of the stalwarts of the GWSR diesel fleet since being returned to traffic in 2013. *Both JW*

TODDINGTON LOCOMOTIVE WORKS: The David Page Locomotive Shed provides the GWSR with a superb facility for maintaining and overhauling its steam locomotive fleet. The four-road depot was funded by a large bequest from the gentleman after whom it is named. Now work on maintaining the fleet can take place all year round, and not be affected by adverse weather conditions. The locomotive department had previously used the old goods shed for such work, but now that has become the machine shop. On 27 October 2018 three of the four running lines are occupied. No 35006 *Peninsular & Oriental S.N. Co* is stabled above the inspection pit to enable work on the leading bogie to take place. To the left is No 2807, undergoing general maintenance, while on the far left is the boiler from BR Standard Class 4 2-6-0 No 76077, the restoration of which is at an early stage. An extension to the rear of this building is planned.

Over the years the GWSR has acquired a range of equipment and machinery to progressively increase its ability both overhaul and restore locomotives. It now has lifting jacks available, and in this view the tender of Great Western 2-8-0 No 3850 has been lifted clear of its wheel sets as part of the ongoing general overhaul of the locomotive. Note, too, the fabricated steel beams on the left, which are part of the new framework for the stairs of the former Henley-in-Arden footbridge at Broadway, necessary due to the poor condition of the originals. *Both JW*

TODDINGTON DIESEL DEPOT: The two road diesel depot, built in 2012, is located next door to the steam depot and workshops, construction having been funded by the diesel locomotive owning groups. Standing on the left-hand road on 29 October 2016 is immaculate No D6948 (later BR Class 37 No 37248), which arrived at Toddington in 2010 and has since received a major overhaul including the fitting of steam heating. Behind is classmate No 37215, while on the right is BR Class 24 No 24081 (D5081), a long-term resident at Toddington since 1981.

On 29 October 2018 a refurbished bogie is seen positioned in front of British Railways Class 24 No 24081 (previously Type 2 No 5081) ready to be wheeled into place beneath the locomotive. The Class 24 is awaiting completion of the refurbishment project, and will hopefully be back in traffic for 2019. On the right is Class 47 No 47105, currently undergoing a major overhaul. *Both JW*

North Gloucestershire Railway

Tucked away on the west side of Toddington station car park is the North Gloucestershire Railway, a 2-foot-gauge (600mm) line that runs for approximately three-quarters of a mile to a point just short of the minor road leading to Didbrook, where a ground frame controls the run-round loop.

The railway dates back to 1962, when it was founded as the Dowty Preservation Society (DPS), located at the Dowty Group's factory in Ashchurch, Gloucestershire, utilising the sidings within the complex, which were connected to the adjacent Birmingham to Bristol main line. In time the DPS hosted a number of then recently preserved main-line locomotives, perhaps the most notable being No 6201 *Princess Elizabeth*. Another interesting, and useful, acquisition was the California Crossing signal box from the closed Eastgate Loop in Gloucester. The group was also the first custodian of Avonside 0-4-0T No 1977 of 1925, better known as *Cadbury No 1*, which following its move to Toddington hauled the first steam services for the then fledgling GWSR.

In 1965 the first narrow-gauge locomotive came to the site, followed in time by others, resulting in a narrow-gauge operation being set up alongside the standard-gauge lines. In addition to locomotives, coaches from various sources also came to the society, thus permitting passenger workings.

In 1982 Dowty gave notice to the DPS that the site was to be redeveloped, thus requiring the society to vacate. Relocation to the present site at Toddington station followed and the DPS set about laying its own line, establishing its main station next to the car park. The new line included the provision of an engine shed and station, which is positioned alongside the GWSR yard and sidings. California Crossing signal box was also resited here, and now lends its name to the narrow-gauge line's intermediate station. Further key events took place in the mid-1980s, as the society changed its name to the North Gloucestershire Railway (NGR) and also disposed of the standard-gauge stock, including *Cadbury No 1*, which is now at Tyseley Locomotive Works in Birmingham.

Further narrow-gauge acquisitions took place and the fleet now has both steam and diesel locomotives available for traffic. It operates between Easter and early September, together with a steam event in October. The journey time is around 25 minutes, which includes calling at California Crossing station to view the engine shed and signal box. This delightful narrow-gauge line complements its bigger neighbour by offering a different experience to passengers as well as providing a fascinating visitor attraction in its own right.

TODDINGTON (NGR): Hunslet 0-4-2T No 6 *Chakas Kraal* departs from the NGR station on 11 September 2016. The loco was built by Hunslet, Works No 2075 of 1940, to an Avonside design for use on the Chakas Krall sugar estates in Natal. It was purchased by the NGR in 1991, and has since spent time on the South Tynedale Railway. *JW*

TODDINGTON (NGR): Ex-German Army 0-8-0T No 1091 approaches Toddington on 2 October 2016 with a return working from Didbrook and California Crossing. This powerful locomotive was built by Henschel & Sohn of Cassel in 1918 (Works No 15968), one of more than 2,000 examples built by several companies for front-line service with the army during the First World War. It later moved to a sugar factory in Poland before being acquired by a group of NGR members in October 1985. The side elevation of the GWSR diesel depot can be seen on the left. *Malcolm Ranieri*

NGR DEPOT: This imposing night scene shows three locomotives in steam and positioned perfectly for photography on 21 October 2017. The line-up consists of, on the left, Polish-built 0-6-0T No 1966 *Tourska*, which was paying a short visit to the line, No 6 *Chakas Kraal* (centre), and Henschel & Sohn No 1091 on the right. *Malcolm Ranieri*

CALIFORNIA CROSSING: A platform is provided here to enable passengers to visit the engine shed and take a look inside the signal box, as well as view the 16mm garden railway positioned next to the signal box. The line to Didbrook is on the west side, and there is a loop on the east side to provide access to the shed. Another evocative night scene on 21 October 2017 has No 6 *Chakas Kraal* standing in the platform at the head of a working for Toddington. The illuminated interior of the signal box and the fallen autumnal leaves add to the atmosphere of the scene. *Malcolm Ranieri*

DIDBROOK: From Toddington to California Crossing the NGR line runs along side the car park and locomotive depots of the GWSR, and it is only after departing from California Crossing that it heads into rural countryside. The southern terminus is the run-round loop at Didbrook, operated by a ground frame; there is no platform here. The end of the line is pictured here on 4 October 2015 as No 1966 *Tourska* heads back to Toddington. There looks to be just enough room to allow *Tourska* to access the turn back siding in the distance, where a wagon has been stabled. *Tourska* was a product of the Fablok Works of Chrzanów, Lesser Poland, built in 1957 (Works No 3512), and spent its early days working at the Dobrzelin sugar factory until 1984, after which it was on display at the Bakkersmollen Museum in Belgium. It came to the UK in 2007 and returned to traffic in 2010, since when it has visited a number of different narrow-gauge systems. *Malcolm Ranieri*

CALIFORNIA CROSSING: On 28 March 2016 *Justine*, an 0-4-0WT (well tank) locomotive, is seen approaching California Crossing from Didbrook. It was constructed by Arnold Jung at the company's works in Kitchen, Germany, in 1906 (Works No 939) and saw service at a Belgian gravel-washing plant at Maeseyck on the River Maas. It came to the UK in 1974 and has since seen service on the Lynton & Barnstaple and Leighton Buzzard railways, as well as returning to Belgium in 1995 for a short stay. It is now out of traffic for its ten-year overhaul. *Malcolm Ranieri*

Hayles Abbey and Winchcombe

HAYLES ABBEY HALT was opened by the GWR on 24 September 1928, reportedly to serve the newly opened museum at nearby Hailes Abbey. The Abbey had been founded in 1246 by Richard, Earl of Cornwall, and was a centre of monastic life for the next three centuries, finally being dissolved in 1539 as a consequence of Dissolution Act of King Henry VIII. The new halt, located 10 miles and 38 chains from Honeybourne East Loop, consisted of two platforms constructed of sleepers, each being provided with a corrugated hut for passenger convenience. Lighting was by oil lamps, which were supervised by staff from nearby Toddington. In the first of the two 'past' views, taken from the west side of the line, GWR '5600' Class 0-6-2T No 5677 heads a southbound freight, then on 21 August 1960, more than five months after closure on 6 March of that year, everything at the halt is still looking pristine, with even the running-in boards still in position.

The site of Hayles Abbey Halt on 5 November 2006 reveals no trace of its existence, as Class 73/1 No 73129, carrying Network SouthEast livery, passes with a southbound working. It has since been repainted into early BR blue and restored to its original number of E6036. *Kidderminster Railway Museum/Roger Carpenter, P. J. Garland collection/JW*

HAYLES ABBEY: Despite the distraction of reinstating the Broadway extension, a small and dedicated team took on the responsibility of rebuilding Hayles Abbey Halt from scratch. It may have taken a couple of years of hard labour, but it was formally reopened on 5 June 2017 and exudes all the atmosphere of a GWR wayside halt. There does not seem to be a definitive reason why the name of the halt and the nearby village and abbey have different spellings – the best answer to date is that it was not uncommon for such things to happen with the GWR! As the new halt caters for a single line, just one platform has been provided and the immaculate corrugated hut was recovered from the long-closed Monmouthshire station of Usk. On a sunny day four months after reopening, No D8137 trundles through heading a southbound service.

The second view is taken from the site of the demolished up platform, roughly where the ramp would have been located. Heading through the reopened station on 14 October 2017 is No 7903 *Foremarke Hall*. The angle of the photograph provides a good view of the front elevation of the former Usk station corrugated hut, as well as the oil lamp suspended on the wooden pole.

The surrounding area has been well manicured, and this view shows the new running-in board at the north end of the platform. An oil lamp is also provided at this end of the platform. Hayles Abbey Halt is a request stop, and on this occasion there were some passengers on board the approaching Class 117 DMU who were no doubt going to spend a pleasant afternoon exploring the nearby countryside and hills. *All JW*

CHICKEN CURVE is situated just north of Winchcombe station, and takes its name from an adjacent chicken farm, now closed. In the past in has been a problematic stretch of line, due to two serious landslips, the first in the early 1920s and the second in January 2011 (see page 64). It is also the point where the Toton to Severn Tunnel Junction freight first became derailed in August 1976 (see page 66), which led to the closure of the line by BR. There is now a 10mph speed restriction on the curve, no doubt as a precaution against any further mishaps. On 28 July 2018 Class 47 No 47376 *Freightliner 1995* approaches the curve along the 'Defford Straight' from Hayles Abbey; the driver is applying power as Winchcombe's signalman has just cleared the Outer Home signal on the approach to the permanent 10mph speed restriction on the curve. The locomotive carries Freightliner grey livery, since replaced on its main-line fleet with green and yellow colours.

The driver of 'Hymek' Class 35 No 7017 is also applying power as he eases his train off the speed restricted section at Chicken Curve, heading for the 'Defford Straight' on 28 July 2018. Originally classified by British Railways as a 'Type 3' locomotive, the 'Hymeks', whose name is derived from its 'Hydraulic Mekydro' transmission, were built by Beyer Peacock in Manchester. *Both JW*

CHICKEN CURVE: The remnants of a heavy Boxing Day snowfall still litter the scene at Chicken Curve on 29 December 2017 as No 7820 *Dinmore Manor* heads for Toddington with a festive season service from Cheltenham Race Course. Langley Hill provides a chilly backdrop, as the wintery sun struggles to make an impact. The extent of the landslip is very evident by the section of the embankment relatively clear of foliage. Note the flattened ridge at the base of the embankment, known as the 'toe berm', which forms a buttress to support it. *JW*

In January 2011, just as the railway was about to recover from the serious landslip at Gotherington, it suffered a further similar event of equal magnitude on the north side of Chicken Curve. Again, the effects of poor drainage off the adjacent Cotswold Hills was the main cause, and resulted in a significant part of the formation becoming dislodged. A similar problem is recorded to have happened in the days of the Great Western Railway during the early 1920s.

The GWSR employed a specialist firm, Ground Investigation & Piling Limited of Wolverhampton (GIP), to fully investigate the problem due to the historic instability in the area. This involved excavating the site to establish the cause of the failure and to recommend the appropriate remedies. Bore holes were drilled and geotechnical equipment installed and monitored, which involved laboratory testing and stability assessments.

GIP then completed the remedial design work and supervised its completion, which included soil nailing to reinforce the embankment and provide future stability, and the use of excavated materials to support the embankment where full reconstruction was not necessary.

As part of the project, the GWSR undertook a review of the drainage around the site, resulting in the clearing and reinforcing of culverts to ensure that water running off the Cotswolds is safely carried away from the railway. The line reopened on 30 October 2012.

CHICKEN CURVE: The first picture shows the beginning of the landslip, evidenced by a dip in the track just beyond the white marker post set in the 'four foot'. That dip soon developed into a serious landslip, which in the second view is being assessed by consultants shortly after the calamitous event. Finally we see the scene today, taken from roughly the same point. *GIP/Jack Boskett/JW*

CHICKEN CURVE: These four images have been kindly provided by Ground Investigation & Piling Limited (GIP), which was engaged by the GWSR to investigate and resolve the issues surrounding the landslip. GIP worked in conjunction with GWSR permanent way staff to fully investigate the site of the landslip and establish the cause of the problem. Piles were then driven into the ground to secure its future integrity before the embankment was reconstructed using granular stone with layers of geotextile. Soil nailing was used to further strengthen the embankment, with excavated materials being used as a 'toe berm' to add support to the embankment, particularly sections not subject to reconstruction.

The first picture shows the embankment being excavated, and the second the excavation and piling completed. Soil nailing is illustrated is the third view, and finally reconstruction of the embankment. *All GIP*

WINCHCOMBE: On 25 August 1976 several wagons in the consist of the 06.35 Toton to Severn Tunnel Junction freight, hauled by Class 45 'Peak' No 45076, derailed on the approach to the main road bridge east of Winchcombe station. The train continued to run for a short distance until the wagons finally left the track where the curvature tightened, next to the down yard. They then spilled over, inflicting severe damage to the track. The first two photographs were taken a few days after the accident, and there appears to have been some clearing up at the site of the derailment, although the derailed train's brake van and one wagon appear to remain in the position where the freight came to grief. In the background is Winchcombe's goods shed.

The goods shed at Winchcombe has seen considerable change since 1976; the original building is now sandwiched by new extensions, and the facility serves as the Carriage & Wagon Works. On 3 September 2016 the Laverton shuttle service, formed of a Class 117 DMU, approaches Winchcombe after having just passed the point where the 1976 derailment took place. *Kidderminster Railway Museum (2)/JW*

WINCHCOMBE CARRIAGE & WAGON WORKS: The important task of restoring and maintaining the fleet of passenger coaches and wagons falls on the dedicated team based at Winchcombe. Originally located in the old goods shed, this has now been extended with the old building now the middle unit between two new extensions. The facility is able to undertake a complete restoration, from overhauling the bogies to attending to wasted wood and metal components through to reupholstering the seating. The shed is in three sections, commencing with the 'stripping down' function at the north (Toddington) end of the works, which incorporates a hoist and jacks that enable coaches to be lifted off their bogies. This set of bogies has recently been released, and their overhaul is about to commence.

(Above right) The stripped down interior is of markI First Only (FO) coach No 3132 that was undergoing restoration in October 2016.

(Below) The same compartment of FO 3132 three years later, now fully restored and returned to traffic. *All JW*

WINCHCOMBE GOODS YARD: Abandoned cars and a boarded-up goods shed are the features at Winchcombe on 24 May 1970 as Type 4 No 1941 (later Class 47/4 No 47498) swings through the site of the station heading a northbound Class 8 freight.

In October 1984 there's a mood of hope and expectation. The track has long since been lifted, but the goods shed is secure and the land is now in the hands of the Gloucestershire Warwickshire Railway, so the task of rebuilding Winchcombe station can begin.

The old goods shed has now been extended to accommodate the Carriage & Wagon Works (see page 67), while the yard has been reinstated and used to store vehicles awaiting restoration or repair. An inspection pit has also been provided. The entrance to the works is on the right, while ex-BR Class 03 No D2182 is ready for shunting duties. *Restoration & Archiving Trust, Tom Cullimore collection/Restoration & Archiving Trust, John Lees collection/JW*

Winchcombe station opened on 1 February 1905 when the line was extended from Toddington, and is exactly 12 miles from Honeybourne East Loop. It is actually situated in the village of Greet, as Winchcombe is some three-quarters of a mile distant. Placed roughly at the mid-point of a long curve, the main station building was located on the down side, with just the customary waiting room on the up side. The signal box was positioned on the down side at the east end of the platform, and the goods shed a short distance further, through which ran a loop line. Three sidings were provided on the down side, behind the goods shed, together with one long siding on the up side that ran for some distance alongside the up platform. Access to the station was by way of a driveway off the road from Greet to Winchcombe; a weighbridge was provided, positioned on the driveway adjacent to the main station building.

Closure to passengers was on 7 March 1960 and to goods on 2 November 1964, with the signal box surviving until 24 February 1965. Following closure, the entire station area was razed to the ground.

The 'new' Winchcombe station was opened by the GWSR on 2 August 1987. The replacement station building had in an earlier life stood at Monmouth Troy, which had been closed in January 1959, and was transported brick-by-brick to Winchcombe and re-erected. Another similar occurrence took place at Winchcombe with the signal box, which was originally located at Hall Green, on the North Warwickshire Line.

MONMOUTH TROY is seen on 3 January 1959, two days before the service between Ross-on-Wye and Chepstow was withdrawn and the station closed. On the right is the 11.00am service from Ross-on-Wye worked by GWR '1400' Class 0-4-2T No 1455, while on the left is GWR '5700' Class 0-6-0PT No 7774, which will go forward to Chepstow. The 'Winchcombe' building is on the left. *Hugh Ballantyne, Rail Photoprints*

WINCHCOMBE: It is June 1987, and progress at Winchcombe is tangible. The station run-round loop is now in situ, and the re-erection of Hall Green signal box has reached a stage where the roof timbers are complete. The symbolic first train from Toddington to reach Winchcombe had operated earlier in the year, on 8 March, 28 years to the day after the withdrawal of passenger services by BR. Scheduled services from Toddington commenced on 2 August 1987.

In a busy scene at Winchcombe, now typical of the current railway, No 7903 *Foremarke Hall* arrives with a service from Toddington on 3 September 2016. Already in the station, waiting for the arrival of the incoming train, is No 35006 *Peninsular & Oriental S.N. Co*, heading a northbound service from Cheltenham Race Course. On the left is the new extension to the goods shed, now serving as the carriage works, and beyond it is the signal box, obscured by the carriage. *Restoration & Archiving Trust, John Lees collection/JW*

WINCHCOMBE: Looking towards Toddington from the now closed station on 24 May 1970, 'Peak' Type 4 No 12 (later Class 45/0 No 45011) rushes by with a southbound express. On the right is the disused goods shed, which was to survive and play a key role in the future development of the heritage line. Note that the 'D' prefix has now been dropped from the locomotive number following the end of steam in 1968.

From the same viewpoint on 12 March 2015, a much different scene is to be witnessed. On the far right is the original goods shed, now extended, which is used for the repair, maintenance and restoration of the railway's fleet of coaches and wagons. The proceedings, which involve No 4270 drawing forward a rake of wagons on 22 March 2015, are being observed by the signalman at the far window of the ex-Hall Green signal box. Coaches awaiting restoration can be seen in the distance. *Kidderminster Railway Museum/JW*

Above: **WINCHCOMBE** station opened on 1 February 1905, and on that day a Great Western steam railmotor is seen standing in the station. The people milling around on the platform, including the crew, perhaps indicate that this was indeed the inaugural working. Steam railmotors were introduced by the GWR to serve its rural, less-populated routes, and consisted of a coach body incorporating a boiler and were thus self-propelled. The design of the boiler is reputed to have earned them the nickname of 'Coffee Pots' on the Honeybourne Line. Designed by Churchward, the first two were introduced in 1903, and during the next five years a further 97 were produced. One of them, No 93, survives and has been restored and returned to traffic in 2011. *Kidderminster Railway Museum*

Opposite: **WINCHCOMBE:** This wonderfully sunny spring morning, highlighting the pristine condition of the buildings at Winchcombe station, is not the joyful occasion it would appear to be. The reason is that the date is 7 March 1960, and this is the last day of the passenger service on the line. A couple run to join the train as the driver looks from his cab awaiting the 'right away' from the guard, which is not yet forthcoming as a member of the station staff seems to be in conversation with someone on the train, probably the guard. This is the 9.40am Honeybourne to Cheltenham St James service, hauled by GWR '9400' Class 0-6-0PT No 8488.

The weather on 22 October 2017 was not quite as good as that fateful spring day in 1960, but there can be genuine joy as trains are, and have been since 1987, again calling at the new Winchcombe station. Standing at roughly the same spot as No 8488 is a Class 117 three-car DMU, which will form the 13.00 service to Toddington and onwards to the then northern limit of the line near to Buckland village. On the far platform a new waiting room has been constructed, similar to the original building except for the traditional roof and platform canopy. *John Stretton/JW*

WAY OUT
OVER FOOTBRIDGE
WINCHCOMBE
WAY OUT

PLATFORM
1
2C36

WINCHCOMBE: This is the view from the up platform as GWR 'Manor' Class 4-6-0 No 7808 *Cookham Manor* approaches heading a charter train for the Stephenson Locomotive Society. The roofs of both the signal box and goods shed can be seen above the train, while on the left is a rake of mineral wagons stabled in the up-side yard.

On 4 April 2014 we see another 'Manor', but more than half a century later. No 7820 *Dinmore Manor*, similarly to No 7808, approaches Winchcombe, now regenerated after the dark years of closure. The 'Great Western' ambiance is there for all to see, and although now in the early years of the 21st century the scene still oozes the atmosphere of a rural station. *Kidderminster Railway Museum/JW*

WINCHCOMBE: In a different viewpoint, from Greet Road bridge, GWR '2251' Class 0-6-0 No 3203 trundles into the station with a northbound engineer's train on 21 August 1960. Although the station has been closed for some months, little seems to have changed. The footbridge remains in situ, as does its roof, while the running-in board still proudly proclaims 'Winchcombe'.

A near timeless scene from the same vantage point of Greet Road bridge is captured on 22 March 2016, as No 4270 heads a demonstration freight through the station. Note that a new, angled running-in board has been provided, and the only noticeable difference between the two images is that the new footbridge does not have a roof. Note, too, that the roof of the now extended goods shed is visible just above the footbridge. *Roger Carpenter, P. J. Garland collection/JW*

WINCHCOMBE: Looking from the foot of the embankment north towards Greet Road bridge on 24 May 1970, English Electric Type 4 No D316 (later Class 40 No 40116) heads south with a coal train, no doubt heading for South Wales. The locomotive carries the early British Railways green livery, which was soon to be supplanted by the ubiquitous Corporate Blue.

The view today has changed little, except that the up line has been removed, and No 7903 *Foremarke Hall* is just passing over the pointwork of the passing loop as it departs from Winchcombe on a very wet 7 July 2012, with a working for Cheltenham Race Course. The signal box and goods shed can just be glimpsed between the roof of the second coach and the underside of the road bridge, while the lineside growth reflects another of our 'warm-wet' summers! *Kidderminster Railway Museum/JW*

WINCHCOMBE: Although not regular visitors, the Western Region diesel-hydraulics did put in an appearance from time to time, usually on race-day specials. However, on 29 March 1975 it was a Plymouth Railway Circle enthusiasts' charter to Derby that brought 'Western' No 1052 *Western Viceroy* to the line, seen here approaching Greet Road bridge with the outward working. In the background is the portal of Greet Tunnel.

The same scene, but seen from Greet Road bridge on 27 August 2008, depicts an even earlier diesel type approaching Winchcombe from Cheltenham Race Course. It is carrying the pre-TOPS No 5580, and when first introduced was classified as a 'Type 2', but following the TOPS renumbering scheme this numerous class of locomotives was redesignated Class 31, this example becoming No 31162. They were a classic mixed-traffic locomotive, although at 109 tons a bit on the heavy side for their power output. The train is just entering the station loop off the single-line section. *Peter Robins/JW*

South of Winchcombe

GREET TUNNEL is one of two major engineering structures on the line, the other being Stanway Viaduct. It is 693 yards long and, because it is on a curve, 'the light at the end of the tunnel' is only visible when reaching each portal. As well as being the second longest tunnel on a heritage railway, the longest being Sharpthorn Tunnel on the Bluebell Railway, some 731 yards long, Greet Tunnel is said to be haunted! The date is August 1985, and although the trackbed had been secured by the GWSR, it was to be another five years before the line was extended through the tunnel at this point to Gretton.

Just 30 years later a pair of Bulleid Southern Railway 'West Country' 'Pacifics' emerge from Greet Tunnel while engaged in a photographers' charter. No 34092 *Wells* leads classmate No 34007 *Wadebridge* on a spirited run-past on 30 May 2015. *Peter Robins/JW*

GREET TUNNEL: The view from above the western portal of the tunnel is stunning, providing a wonderful vista across Gloucestershire to the River Severn and beyond. On the left is the dominating presence of the 734-foot Oxenton Hill, which sets the scene, with the distant Malvern Hills forming an impressive backdrop. The lengthening shadows indicate that this is an autumnal afternoon, but it is also noticeable that there is little evidence of the leaves falling despite the date being 29 October 2017. Approaching is 'Peak' Class 45/1 No 45149 with a service for Toddington. *JW*

GRETTON HALT was situated on an embankment on the Gotherington side of the bridge that carries the line over the road to Winchcombe, some 13 miles and 36 chains from Honeybourne East Loop. It was provided with two 100-foot wooden platforms, later extended by a further 50 feet, each with a 'Pagoda' waiting shelter. A local request for a siding to serve the nearby farmers had been refused by the GWR prior to the line being opened, but the provision of a halt was agreed and it opened on 1 June 1906. It was under the jurisdiction of the station master at Winchcombe, and served not only Gretton but also nearby Stanley Pontlarge, the latter being notable as the home at one time of well-known railway author L. T. C. Rolt. The halt closed on 7 March 1960, upon withdrawal of the passenger service.

Nothing remains of the halt today, and the only way to pinpoint its location is to note the girders of the road bridge beneath the third coach of the approaching train, which can be tied in to the same girders in the earlier picture. This view approximates roughly with the position of the up platform. Passing the site is No 7903 *Foremarke Hall* on a wet 30 March 2018. *W. A. Camwell, Maurice Dart collection/JW*

DIXTON CUTTING: The ruling adverse gradient northwards from Hunting Butts Tunnel, beyond Cheltenham Race Course, was steady, but unremitting, with a maximum gradient of 1 in 150, but mostly of the order of 1 in 200. The summit was north of Gotherington, where the line levelled out towards Gretton Halt. The final stretch of the climb passed through the shallow and wide Dixton Cutting, and this late-1960s view shows British Railways Type 4 No D1612 (later Class 47 No 47479) speeding towards Gotherington with a diverted southbound express. The change of gradient can be clearly seen in the background.

The best part of 30 years separate the second view from the first. In that time the line has been closed and the track torn up. But now that process is in reverse, and in the spring of 1996 track-laying in Dixton Cutting is under way ahead of the reopening of the line to Gotherington the following year. Ex-British Railways diesel-mechanical 0-6-0 shunter No 2182, later to become a Class 03, is sandwiched between two bolster wagons carrying rail and a trio of vans attached to a brake van. There is evidence of much cutting back of trees to open up the view. The power cables in the background provide a point of reference.

There has been little change at Dixton Cutting over the ensuing years, as illustrated by the scene on 9 December 2017 with No D6948 heading for Cheltenham Race Course with empty coaching stock for a Santa Special. *Pete Evans, Jack Boskett collection/The Restoration & Archiving Trust, GWR collection/JW*

Gotherington

Gotherington station opened on 1 June 1906, 15 miles and 33 chains from Honeybourne East Junction. The main station building was on the up (northbound) side, with a waiting shelter on the down side. A small goods shed was positioned at the south end of the up platform, and the associated goods yard consisted of a single siding leading from a loop off the up line. The original signal box was positioned to the south of the up platform.

Traffic does not appear to have lived up to the GWR's expectations, as goods facilities ceased in 1949, and the signal box closed on 3 April of that year, together with the goods siding and connections. The station had earlier been reduced to the status of a 'halt' in 1941, and on 13 June 1955 closed altogether.

After closure the down platform was demolished, but on the up side the station building was retained and for a period let to railway employees. Cost-cutting by BR resulted in the removal of the up platform and part of the canopy, and in 1978 the building was sold. Once in private hands the new owner built a large two-storey extension between the station building and goods shed, as well as removing other features associated with the past.

In 1981 all was to change, as the building was acquired by the present occupier, Bryan Nicholls, who set about the daunting task of restoring the station to its former glory. It is a huge understatement just to say he is responsible for the magnificent restored station that can be seen today. Fortunately, his vivid account of the trials and tribulations of this task can be found in 'Railways & Recollections' No 39, *Gotherington Station*, published by Silver Link (ISBN: 978 1 85794 421 1).

GOTHERINGTON STATION: A view off the privately owned former 'Up' platform at Gotherington, as No. 4270 approaches with a freight working during a photographers charter on 22 March 2016. *JW* (with permission)

GOTHERINGTON station is seen on 31 August 1962 as GWR 'Castle' 4-6-0 No 7026 *Tenby Castle* hurries through with the Penzance portion of the up 'Cornishman'. Nothing remains of the down platform, and even the trees that fringed the platform have been chopped down, leaving just a line of stumps to mark their passing. The station had been closed for more than seven years at this point, but the television aerial affixed to a chimney confirms its change of use to a domestic dwelling house.

Nineteen years later, in August 1981, the station building remains intact, with many original features still very much in evidence. Note that the chimney pots remain, although the television aerial has gone. This view shows graphically how the canopy was hacked back by BR, although the down pipe on the side elevation remains in position. The main difference is the two-storey extension that adjoins the original building, constructed prior to Bryan Nicholls's tenure.

On 30 March 2018 No 2807 works through the station non-stop with a service for Broadway. Today both platforms have been reinstated, with a small brick waiting shelter available for GWSR passengers. On the right, the restoration of the old station building is complete with the surrounding pine trees masking the impact of the new extension. All the paraphernalia of a GWR station is there to see, from running-in boards and spiked railings to the station clock and signage. *The Restoration & Archiving Trust, John Dagley Morris collection/ Bryan Nicholls/JW*

GOTHERINGTON is seen again in the late 1960s, showing the station and the small goods shed with its gabled roof. Part of the up platform remains, serving as a 'patio' for the residents of the old station building, albeit now separated from the railway by a fence. Nothing remains of the down platform, the site of which has been reclaimed by nature. The line is now the preserve of diesels, and an unidentified Brush Type 4 (Class 47) is seen passing through with an express heading for the South West.

The same view in August 1981 shows clearly the new 'extension', sandwiched between the goods shed, now with patio doors, and the old station building. The canopy has been cut back while the trackbed is now a river of spent ballast.

The scene today reveals a mature station, with Birmingham Railway Carriage & Wagon Co Type 2 No D5343 (later Class 25 No 26004) standing in the platform with a train for Cheltenham Race Course. The locomotive spent most of its working life in Scotland, but is now enjoying a second career in the Cotswolds. The old station has been superbly restored, with its ambience enhanced by a selection of old railway artefacts including enamel advertising signs, goose-neck lamps, fire buckets and notices. Both platforms have been reconstructed by owner Bryan Nicholls, while the GWSR later provided the new waiting shelter, which blends into the scene well. *W. Potter, Bryan Nicholls collection/Bryan Nicholls/JW*

GOTHERINGTON: This was Gotherington in 1932, looking towards Cheltenham, showing the main station building on the up side and the small waiting shelter opposite. Of particular note, though, is that the photograph shows the position of the signal box on the up side just off the platform end. It was an early casualty, as the goods facilities did not meet expectations and, together with the goods sidings, it was taken out of use in April 1949 and subsequently demolished.

The desolate scene in November 1984 has a silver lining: reconstruction of the up platform has just been completed, and work on restoring the down platform is soon to start. What looks like a GWR goose-neck lamp post stands forlornly at the far end of the platform, but its future was bright!

From roughly the same spot in 2015 the scene is complete, even with that goose-neck lamp post now in pride of place at the end of the restored up platform. On this sunny day at the end of December, the down platform is in shade, but the period bench and new waiting shelter, clad in Cotswold stone, finish off the scene well. A group of three await the arrival of Class 37 No 37215, but will first have to wait for the signalman to exchange the token with the driver. The new GWSR signal box, now known as 'Gotherington West', is located next to the entrance to the old goods yard, and it is a joy to view the many items of railwayana on display. *R. S. Carpenter, Clarence Gilbert collection/Bryan Nicholls/JW*

GOTHERINGTON: These two views of Gotherington were taken 20 years apart bar a few days. The first shows a scene of activity on a bright sunny Christmas Day 1995, looking north along the embankment towards the station, which can be seen in the background. On the immediate left are the remains of the cattle dock, which will later be removed by the GWSR to create space for its new signal box. Next is the entrance to the old goods yard, while work on the trackbed is progressing towards the reopening that took place two years later.

By way of contrast, on 29 December 2015 the goods yard has now been redeveloped and the siding restored, albeit disconnected from the main line. On the left is 'Gotherington West Shunt Frame' cabin. Approaching is No 45149 piloting No 7820 *Dinmore Manor* on a service for Cheltenham Race Course. The crew of the diesel are looking out for the signalman with the single-line token for exchange, which will actually be completed by the fireman on No 7820, who can also be seen leaning from the cab. The track immediately to the left of the train is Gotherington Loop. *Bryan Nicholls/JW*

GOTHERINGTON WEST is not part of the GWSR, but a private development created by Bryan Nicholls, which complements perfectly the work he has undertaken on refurbishing the station building and platforms. It stands on land once occupied by the goods yard, which closed in 1949, and is aimed at replicating the atmosphere of a GWR wayside halt. The full story can be found in Silver Link's 'Railways & Recollections' No 39, and is an essential read.

The 'Pagoda' shelter (previously standing at Willersey Halt) seen in the first view, presents a contrasting view to the main-line signal box, which was built on the site of the old cattle dock. The position of the signal box renders any future main -line connection difficult.

The resited cattle dock is now at the end of the short line running from Gotherington West platform, which can just be seen on the extreme left. The original cattle dock was demolished to make way for the GWSR signal box.

The 'new' Gotherington Signal Box, seen in the third picture, stands on the foundations of the original, which closed in 1949, and is constructed of reclaimed original railway materials. It is positioned on the up side, just inside the boundary fence.

The system has its own motive power, an ex-Wickham powered two-seater, purchased in a stripped-down condition and now restored. It is housed in its own shed, code 85N! *All JW, with permission from Bryan Nicholls*

GOTHERINGTON LOOP: Because the original station building on the up side at Gotherington is in private hands, since the GWSR extended to Gotherington its services have used the old down platform. Later, when the line was extended further to Cheltenham Race Course, it was decided to construct a passing loop to the south of Gotherington station, which meant that especially on gala days a more intensive service could be operated. A signal box was constructed to control the new loop, but its opening was delayed by a serious landslip roughly midway along the loop, which severed the line between Gotherington and Cheltenham Race Course and followed a similar, but less extensive, landslip near Cheltenham two years earlier. An appeal launched by the new President of the GWSR, Pete Waterman, raised more than £1 million, the repairs were completed and services recommenced in 2011. In September 2010 Pete Waterman stands next to the formation of the Up Loop, now suspended in mid-air following the collapse of the embankment.

The area on the left clear of bushes pinpoints the location of the 2010 embankment collapse. The embankment was subject to extensive reconstruction as well as completely refurbishing and renewing the culverts to ensure that water running off the nearby Cotswold Hills would not cause further damage. In March 2012 No 4270 passes over the stretch of line affected by the landslip. *Both JW*

GOTHERINGTON LOOP: Gotherington Signal Box is located at the north end of the loop, where up trains are held awaiting the passage of down workings to Cheltenham Race Course. An intensive post-Christmas service was operating on 29 December 2015, necessitating the use of the loop. The bright winter sunshine can be seen glinting off the coaches of the southbound service through the bushes on the left, while No 5542 awaits the single-line token to Winchcombe and the Inner Home signal to be cleared prior to continuing through to Toddington.

At the south end of Gotherington Loop, protected by the Outer Home bracket signals, No 70013 *Oliver Cromwell* works off the Down Loop with a service for Cheltenham Race Course on a damp and grey 28 May 2018. The train is just passing over the section affected by the 2010 embankment collapse. 'Britannia' 'Pacifics' were frequent visitors to the line, usually hauling summer Saturday workings between the West Midlands and South Coast holiday resorts in the early 1960s. *Both JW*

MANOR LANE, GOTHERINGTON: Having just passed through Gotherington, an unidentified Brush Type 4 with a southbound express speeds round the gentle curve where the line crosses Manor Lane, having just worked over what will in future become the GWSR passing loop. The mix of blue and grey with maroon stock dates this image to the mid- to late-1960s. Oxenton Hill forms an impressive backdrop.

One of the visitors to the GWSR 2018 Steam Gala was ex-United States Army Transportation Corps (USATC) 'S160' Class 2-8-0 No 5197. These locomotives were constructed during the Second World War and saw service both in the UK and Europe, prior to being dispersed around the globe in the post-war era; No 5197 subsequently worked for the Chinese State Railway before being repatriated to the UK. Indeed, members of the class have worked along the Honeybourne Line on freight services. On 28 May 2018 Nos 5197 and 35006 *Peninsular & Oriental S.N. Co* have just passed over Manor Lane with the 09.40 Toddington-Cheltenham Race Course service. *Restoration & Archiving Trust, John Dagley Morris collection/JW*

MANOR LANE, GOTHERINGTON: South of Gotherington Loop there is a mile-long straight section of track, which has a ruling gradient of 1 in 150 against northbound trains. The gradient is emphasised in this long telephoto shot from Manor Lane looking south towards Bishop's Cleeve, where the station site can be identified as being between the distant large conifer trees. Approaching Gotherington Loop's fixed Distant signal is GWR 'King' Class 4-6-0 No 6023 *King Edward II* heading a service for Broadway on 10 June 2018. It is carrying 'The Red Dragon' headboard, which was a named British Railways express operating between London Paddington, Swansea and Carmarthen from 1950 until 1965. *JW*

Bishop's Cleeve: Here is a different, and striking, perspective of the stretch of line between Bishop's Cleeve and Manor Lane, taken on 4 March 2017. A shaft of sunlight pierces the cloud to illuminate No 2807 as it works up the 1 in 150 gradient with a northbound service. Note the encroachment of residential development, no doubt due to Bishop Cleeve's close proximity to Cheltenham, including a substantial new estate on the right that will change this viewpoint for ever. *Ralph Ward*

Bishop's Cleeve station opened on 1 June 1906, 16 miles and 76 chains from Honeybourne East Loop. The main station building was situated on the up side, with a waiting shelter provided on the down side. The signal box, which was clad in Cotswold stone, was positioned to the south of the station on the down side and adjacent to the goods yard, which consisted of a loop that also served the goods shed, together with three sidings. The station closed on 7 March 1960, predating the demise of the goods yard, which closed on 1 July 1963.

In his illustrated history of the line (Irwell Press, 1994), Audie Baker describes a tragic incident that occurred at Bishop's Cleeve in August 1928. The station did not have a footbridge, so passengers and staff had to use the barrow crossing to cross the running lines. Two sisters were using the barrow crossing on that fateful day when they were mown down by an express. It is believed that they had mistaken the oncoming train as their stopping service. A verdict of accidental death was recorded.

Bishop's Cleeve station is seen here when new, with a Great Western railmotor standing in the down platform forming a Honeybourne-Cheltenham 'Coffee Pot' service. Just beyond the train is the bridge that carries the railway over a road, beyond which there is a long section of straight track, mostly on an embankment, which leads to Gotherington. The outline of Oxenton Hill can be seen in the background. *Lens of Sutton*

Bishop's Cleeve: On 5 March 1960, two days before the withdrawal of passenger services by BR, No 8488 departs with a Honeybourne to Cheltenham St James service. In the foreground is the connection to the goods yard, to the left of which is the head shunt.

There is now little to suggest that a station once stood at this point except for some paving slabs that are virtually hidden in the undergrowth to the left. The girders of Station Road bridge can be seen to the left of No 5542, which is approaching with a Halloween 'Spooky Special' on 31 October 2015. The 25mph speed limit sign is an indicator of roughly where the platform end was located. As can be seen, the location is now hemmed in by rapid tree growth that shields the railway from the ribbon housing development on both sides of the line. Gotherington's fixed Distant signal can be seen in the background. *Kidderminster Railway Museum, W. Potter collection/JW*

Bishop's Cleeve: In another view of Bishop's Cleeve Halt, this time looking south, the signal box and goods shed can be seen beyond the rear of passing Class 122 'Bubble Car' No 55004 on 24 July 1965. The unit is operating a Gloucester Central to Leamington Spa service, which although not calling at stations south of Honeybourne, did serve those on the line to Stratford-upon-Avon, which did not lose its passenger service until the following year. The station is derelict, looking as though it has been ransacked, while part of the platform has been removed. Note, too, that the down platform has already been demolished.

Looking at the same location today, but from the trackbed of the now lifted up line, the GWSR single line is at this point laid along the formation of the old down line. The train is running past what would have been the down platform, with the site of the main station building on the extreme right of the picture. The girders are those of the Station Road bridge, while visiting Ivatt Class 2MT 2-6-0 No 46521 is heading a northbound demonstration freight towards Winchcombe on 30 May 2016. *Kidderminster Railway Museum, W. Potter collection/JW*

Bishop's Cleeve's distinctive signal box is the feature of this view, unusual in that it was clad in Cotswold stone. It was a GWR Type 27 box, and dates back to the opening of the line. It was closed on 11 August 1965, from which date the block section was extended from Toddington to Malvern Road East, Cheltenham. A few weeks later, on 4 September, BR 'Britannia' 'Pacific' No 70053 *Moray Firth* approaches the now closed signal box heading a summer Saturday express from Wolverhampton to the South Coast.

Fifty-three years later, on 3 June 2018 to be exact, a 'Britannia' can once again be seen at Bishop's Cleeve. No 70013 *Oliver Cromwell* is passing through the site of the old station with a working from Broadway to Cheltenham Race Course. The view, however, has changed beyond all recognition, as the line is now singled, and the station buildings, platforms and signals box have all long since been demolished. A new housing development occupies part of the goods yard close to the running lines – so close in fact that the GWSR has installed continuous welded rail at this point to minimise the noise. *Kidderminster Railway Museum, W. Potter collection/JW*

Bishop's Cleeve: The line was built to accommodate fast express workings, and these continued well beyond the withdrawal of the stopping passenger service in 1960. The last steam-hauled summer Saturday working took place on 4 September 1965, and on that day 'Britannia' No 70045 *Lord Rowallan* is seen charging past the now closed goods yard and signal box at Bishop's Cleeve with a working from the South Coast to Wolverhampton. By this time most of the track in the goods yard, which had closed on 1 July 1963, had been torn up.

Just an avenue of trees marks the spot nowadays, as No 35006 *Peninsular & Oriental S.N. Co* approaches with a Cheltenham Race Course to Toddington working on 30 May 2016. The abbreviated initials on the locomotive's nameplate indicated that there was insufficient space to carry the full name of the shipping line, which was 'Peninsular & Oriental Steam Navigation Company'. *Kidderminster Railway Museum, W. Potter collection/JW*

Bishop's Cleeve: There is no trace remaining to indicate that this was once the station goods yard. The photographer, whose shadow can be seen in the bottom right-hand corner, is standing at the southern end of what was the goods yard. The new housing and social club (extreme left) now occupy part of the site, with what looks like an Austin A30 in the car park. Passing is a truly mixed freight of vans, cement and mineral wagons, heading no doubt for South Wales behind English Electric Type 1s Nos D8189 and D8167 (later Class 20s Nos 20189 and 20167) on a sunny 20 December 1970.

The view on 29 October 2017 shows No 45149 passing with the 13.30 Toddington-Cheltenham Race Course working. On the left the fence posts seem to have survived the intervening 47 years, although there are some changes to the buildings now occupying the site of the goods yard. The single-storey property seems to have been removed, while the social club looks to have had a make-over. If ever the GWSR was to consider reinstating a station at Bishop's Cleeve, this would be the most likely location. *The Restoration & Archiving Trust, Tom Cullimore collection/JW*

Bishop's Cleeve: On 25 July 1964 GWR 'Castle' Class No 7011 *Banbury Castle* approaches Two Hedges Road bridge in Bishop's Cleeve while heading a Wolverhampton to Penzance express. Note the goods shed at Bishop's Cleeve, which can be seen above the last coach of the train.

Forty-nine years later, on 1 September 2013, No 5542 approaches with a southbound working. While this is a narrower viewpoint than that in 1964, the roofline of the houses confirms the location. The site of the goods yard can be seen beyond the train, although the goods shed has long since gone, now replaced by the social club and new housing estate. *The Restoration & Archiving Trust, Tony Bowles/JW*

SOUTHAM ROAD: The view to the south from the road bridge is perhaps one of the most familiar on the line, as it looks towards Cheltenham Race Course station, which is tucked away in the distance. To the left is the racecourse itself, of world renown for its annual spring meeting and the classic race, the Cheltenham Gold Cup. But it is also a place where the iron horse competes with the racehorse for attention, since 1906 when the railway from Cheltenham to Honeybourne opened. The rundown of steam traction on British Railways is reflected in this 1 June 1965 scene as BR Standard Class 5 4-6-0 No 73034 approaches Southam Road with a rake of empty mineral wagons, probably returning from South Wales.

By 1967 the line was fully dieselised, and on 10 September of that year 'Peak' Type 4 No D81 (later Class 45/1 No 45115) is seen working north with a diverted express. In this view the platforms of the Race Course station can clearly be seen in the cutting, while the racecourse itself is concealed behind the line of trees to the left of the platforms. *John Stretton/The Restoration & Archiving Trust, Tom Cullimore collection*

SOUTHAM ROAD: By 2006 the view of Cheltenham Race Course station has been completely obscured by trees, but judging by the cars parked on the hill a function is in progress at the racecourse itself. However, the action is certainly railway-based, as the heritage line was operating a late-season diesel gala on 5 November of that year. English Electric Class 37 No 37324 *Clydebridge* makes a noisy departure from the Race Course station as it powers around the curve on the approach to Southam Road. On the right the arable farming has been turned over to the stabling of horses, whose apparent lack of interest in the growling Class 37 suggests that they have become used to the passing 'iron horses'!

It looks to be another busy day both at the racecourse and on the railway, as visiting GWR 'King' No 6023 *King Edward II* certainly brings out the crowds to mark its visit to the GWSR on a wonderfully sunny 3 June 2018. The driver has just opened the regulator as the train sweeps off the curve towards the road bridge. *Both JW*

Cheltenham Race Course

The popularity of horse-racing and the presence of Cheltenham racecourse close to the Honeybourne Line were the dominant factors that led to the opening of a station here to serve the race-goers. Cheltenham Race Course station opened on 12 March 1912, and was notable for its two long 700-foot, 15-foot wide platforms, designed to accommodate the anticipated crowds using the special race-day trains. In fact, the down platform was later extended by a further 260 feet at the south end. Access to the platforms was by means of quite steep footpaths from the roadway above. A signal box was situated on the up side just beyond the northern end of the platform.

As the station's sole purpose was to serve the racecourse, it had no scheduled services and only opened on race days with a regular pattern of workings, consisting of around half a dozen specials arriving at the station from each direction. The stock from these trains would be distributed in goods yards along the line, with the locomotives often going some distance to be serviced. Additionally, the local service also called at the station on race days.

During wartime race meetings were suspended, so the station was effectively closed from April 1915 until May 1919, then again from March 1942 until March 1945. However, due to its role of serving race-goers it survived the mass closures in March 1960, when the local passenger service was withdrawn, but ultimately succumbed to the impact of increased use of the motor car by race-goers and was closed on 25 March 1968. However, this decision was reversed three years later, when it reopened for the March meeting and remained so until August 1976 when, together with the line, it was closed due to the Winchcombe derailment. On 7 April 2003 it was again reopened, this time by the GWSR, and now serves as the railway's southern terminus.

CHELTENHAM RACE COURSE: The 'new' GWSR station here replicates much of the original. In the background is the A435 main road bridge, and a new shop, cafe and toilet block have been provided on the down platform. The up platform has also now been restored, but is not yet in general use. A new signal box stands in the position once occupied by the original structure. Approaching with a returning Santa Special from Winchcombe on 9 December 2017 is visiting GWR '4500' Class 2-6-2T 'Prairie' No 5526, which is normally based on the South Devon Railway. *JW*

CHELTENHAM RACE COURSE: In 1998 a section of track was laid between the platforms to promote a share issue, but the actual GWSR running line did not reach the station until 28 December 2000. Two days later, after a gap of 25 years, the first train worked into the station, consisting of a permanent way working hauled by BR Class 03 0-6-0DM shunter No D2182. The train is seen standing in the up platform, which is now used as the run-round loop. Of note, the up platform survived closure, whereas the down platform had been demolished.

It was to take a further couple of years to bring the 3-mile extension from Gotherington to the Race Course station up to operating standard, which involved the laying of 8,000 tonnes of stone ballast. The fruition of all this work came on 17 November 2002 with the arrival of the first train with passenger coaching stock since the last race special in 1976, hauled by GWR 'Modified Hall' Class 4-6-0 No 6960 *Raveningham Hall*. Of equal importance, though, was that it was the formal launch of an important future partnership between the railway and the racing fraternity to run race-day specials for race-goers from Toddington, avoiding the problems of chronic congestion and parking if travelling by car to Cheltenham on race days. The launch train is seen standing in the reinstated down platform, while GWR '6400' Class 0-6-0 pannier tank No 6412 waits in the up platform. *The Restoration & Archiving Trust, Andrew Manley/JW*

CHELTENHAM RACE COURSE: It's the end of an era as the last steam-hauled 'Gold Cup Special' from London Paddington simmers in the station on 14 March 1963, hauled by GWR 'Castle' Class 4-6-0 No 7029 *Clun Castle*. Diesel-hauled specials were to continue until 1976. Note the black shutters that were used to protect the windows of the signal box from unwanted attention when it was switched out. *Clun Castle* was withdrawn from BR service in December 1965 and subsequently acquired by Patrick Whitehouse to become the flagship locomotive of the Birmingham Railway Museum based at Tyseley, under whose stewardship it then enjoyed an illustrious continued main-line presence for many years. In fact, *Clun Castle* has just re-emerged after a lengthy overhaul and will again grace the main line in 2019.

The signal box closed in February 1964 and was subsequently demolished. It was replaced by the GWSR in 2005 with a new structure to control movements in and around the station, which had reopened two years earlier. The new signal box is clad in bricks reflecting the shade of the local Cotswold stone, and makes an impressive sight in this view with No 35006 *Peninsular & Oriental S.N. Co* standing alongside on 3 September 2016. *Kidderminster Railway Museum, W. Potter collection/JW*

CHELTENHAM RACE COURSE: Looking towards the A435 Evesham Road bridge on 18 June 1967, 'Peak' Type 4 No D16 (later Class 45/0 No 45011) rushes through the station with a northbound express. On the left is the pathway that leads to the booking office alongside the main road, while the access ramp from the roadway to the up platform can be seen behind the running-in board. In the distance, looking through the arch of the bridge, is the northern portal of Hunting Butts Tunnel.

A closer view shows the end of the run-round loop beyond the main road bridge. The track then continues to a point close to the northern portal of Hunting Butts Tunnel, which is used as a storage siding for various items of stock. On 17 November 2002 No 6412 is heading a short freight train. Note the newly installed water tank on the left. *Kidderminster Railway Museum/JW*

CHELTENHAM RACE COURSE: Light and shade provide an atmospheric scene on 31 October 2015 as No D8137 runs round its train. The northern portal of Hunting Butts Tunnel can just be seen in the far distance through the arch of the main road bridge. At the top of the cutting, top left, is the booking office, while at platform level the renovation work on the water tower is much in evidence. *JW*

1M50

CHELTENHAM RACE COURSE: This view of the station when first opened is looking from the down platform towards Toddington. Of immediate note is the lack of mature trees, which indicates that this view probably dates to around the time the station opened in 1912, and the Corsican pines that dominate the scene today are still little more than saplings. Each platform was provided with an attractively designed waiting room that included toilet facilities for the racegoers. Nothing more was required as the station catered exclusively for passengers heading either to or from the racecourse. In the background is the signal box.

By way of contrast to the neat and tidy appearance of the station when new, the second view, taken in July 1968, shows its decline with the platforms becoming infested with weeds and self-setting plants. The platform facilities have been removed, the only remnant of better days being the running-in board on the down platform. The ramp to the roadway can be seen just beyond the solitary figure in the background. The station had been formally closed earlier in 1968, hence its unkempt state, but was to reopen to serve race specials in 1971 through to the line's closure in 1976.

The general view of the reopened station on 8 August 2016 shows No 35006 *Peninsular & Oriental S.N. Co* in the down platform awaiting departure with a charter working. On the right progress is being made with the reinstatement of the up platform, which will eventually provide the GWSR with greater flexibility, especially when dealing with race-day specials. *Kidderminster Railway Museum/John Stretton/JW*

CHELTENHAM RACE COURSE: The view from the A435 road bridge on 30 May 2016 shows No 7820 *Dinmore Manor* standing in Platform 1, having just arrived with a service from Toddington. In the foreground is the impressive water tank and hose, to replenish the tanks of thirsty steam locomotives. Note that the project to reinstate the second platform is at an advanced stage, while the signal box is just visible in the background, partly hidden by the huge Corsican pine trees that border the station. *JW*

CHELTENHAM RACE COURSE: The station's booking office has been a feature of the locality since the station opened in 1912, and is thought to be the last surviving example of a prefabricated building, the component parts of which were manufactured at Swindon Works and then transported by train to be erected on site. It also survived the subsequent neglect and attention of local vandals during its period of closure, to enter a new era when the GWSR reopened the station in 2003. It has since been fully restored and, due to its prominent position alongside the busy main road, also serves as a wonderful advertisement for the heritage railway. The first view shows the building in August 1977, and the second the now fully renovated building on 31 October 2015. *Kidderminster Railway Museum/JW*

HUNTING BUTTS TUNNEL: To the south of Cheltenham Race Course station is the 97-yard-long Hunting Butts Tunnel. It is suggested that it was originally planned to run the line through a cutting at this point, but apparently the racecourse owners objected as it would interfere with their gallops, and a tunnel was constructed. The GWSR owns the trackbed to a point beyond the now boarded-up southern portal of the tunnel, and use the track south of Race Course station as storage sidings. Looking from the A435 road bridge, a diverted non-stop northbound express hauled by 'Peak' Type 4 No D58 *The King's Own Royal Border Regiment* (later Class 45/0 No 45043) speeds from the tunnel and approaches the road bridge and Cheltenham Race Course station. The 'Peak' is carrying the 'new' British Rail Corporate Blue livery (the early lighter shade version) and nine of the 11 coaches also carry the Corporate blue and grey colours, which suggests that the picture was taken in the late 1960s.

The view from the road bridge on 22 October 2017 sees No 35006 *Peninsular & Oriental S.N. Co* in the process of running round its train. In the distance can be seen the northern portal of the tunnel, but the main feature of this scene is the abundant tree growth that has taken place in the intervening years. *Pete Evans, Jack Boskett collection/JW*

HUNTING BUTTS TUNNEL: An unidentified 'Peak' Type 4 has just emerged from the southern portal of the tunnel and heads for Lansdown Junction with a diverted southbound express. The date is unknown, but most likely during the late 1960s.

In December 2017, viewed from Swindon Lane bridge, the course of the line can be seen as can part of the southern portal of the tunnel, but all is now hemmed in by the unrestricted growth of lineside vegetation. The GWSR's southern boundary is just south of this point. *Pete Evans, Jack Boskett collection/JW*

Cheltenham stations

Cheltenham now has just one station serving the town, Lansdown Road on the former Midland cross-country main line from Birmingham to Bristol. Once it had four, the others being St James, Malvern Road and High Street. Lansdown Road station opened in 1840, but was, and is, remote from the town centre. Seven years later a new station was opened near St James Square, then known as just 'Cheltenham', which was close to the town centre and served GWR services on its newly opened line via Stroud to Swindon. In 1894 the original was replaced by a new station, initially again called 'Cheltenham', but later having the words 'St James' added. When the Honeybourne Line opened in 1906 trains from the north initially had to reverse at Malvern Road East Signal Box to gain access to St. James until provision of the bay platform at the new Malvern Road station for this very purpose. High Street Halt, which opened in 1908 and was located to the north of Malvern Road, had a brief life of just nine years. There was also another High Street station, situated on the Midland line north of Lansdown Road, which opened in 1862 and closed in 1910.

After the Honeybourne Line closed in 1976, the trackbed was protected to the GWSR boundary at a point just south of Hunting Butts Tunnel, and converted into a footpath and cycleway that now continues through to a point close to Lansdown Road station.

HIGH STREET HALT: This photograph of the halt is thought to be the only one in existence and shows a steam railmotor approaching from Honeybourne. The halt opened on 1 October 1908 and had just a short lifespan of nine years, closing on 30 April 1917 as a wartime economy measure, but not reopened after the end of hostilities. It consisted of two platforms constructed from what appears to be wooden railway sleepers, with a GWR-pattern 'Pagoda' waiting shelter provided on each platform. The train is crossing the bridge that spans High Street.

The location is now part of the Cheltenham 'Honeybourne Line' path and cycleway that follows the course of the closed railway. Access to the station site is now through the Winston Churchill Memorial Garden, which connects with the pathway at a point close to the position of the 'Pagoda' shelter. The parapet and girders of the High Street road bridge pinpoint the location of the old station, while the footpath continues north from High Street for a further half-mile to the Prince of Wales stadium. *Lens of Sutton/JW*

MALVERN ROAD EAST JUNCTION: Originally known as the 'Cheltenham Branch', the line from Swindon and Stroud ran directly into the GWR station, which later became known as St James. The opening of the Honeybourne Line created a junction, just north of Malvern Road East Signal Box (the successor to an earlier signal box known as Bayshill that was demolished to make way for the new Honeybourne Line). Initially a double-track formation, it later expanded to provide double-track leads to both St James station and the Honeybourne Line, a project that also caused the engine shed to be relocated. Before the opening of Malvern Road, Honeybourne Line trains had to reverse just before Malvern Road East Signal Box to operate to and from St James station. The junction is spanned by St Georges Road bridge, and looking down from the bridge on 9 August 1962 GWR 'Manor' Class 4-6-0 No 7805 *Broome Manor* has just passed Malvern Road East Signal Box, on the left, and is taking the spur into St James. Malvern Road station platform can just be seen through the arch of the background bridge.

The scene today still reflects the old junction layout, albeit now with the footpath and cycleway denoting the respective routes. *Restoration & Archiving Trust, Richard Dagley Morris collection/JW*

CHELTENHAM SPA ST JAMES: The approach and layout at St James was extensive, with a raft of sidings for goods traffic on both sides of the main line into the station. The most extensive was on the south side, with a fan of eight roads together with a goods shed positioned at the side off the passenger station. On a wet and grim 11 November 1961 GWR '2251' Class 0-6-0 No 2241 departs with the 11.45am service to London Paddington, which will reverse at Gloucester Central, and no doubt re-engine for something a bit more powerful. Note the signal box in the left background.

Although nothing remains of the station, its position can always be pinpointed by the spire of St Gregory's church, as it is in this view looking down from St Georges Road through the gap beside the modern apartment block on the site of the line into the station. *Restoration & Archiving Trust, Richard Dagley Morris Collection/JW*

CHELTENHAM SPA ST JAMES: This is a fascinating view of St James Square taken some time after 1901, which was the opening date of the Cheltenham & District Light Railway electric tram system; It survived until the end of 1930. The only remaining relic is an English Electric-built single-deck tram, No 21, which is owned by the Cheltenham Trust. Services ran from Lansdown Road to Cleeve Hill, Prestbury, Charlton Kings and Leckhampton. One of the company's open-top trams is seen making its way through St James Square along a road shared only with a couple of people on bicycles. On the right is the distinctive spire of the Roman Catholic Church of St Gregory the Great, which stands opposite the impressive frontage of the new station that replaced the original in September 1894. Until 1908 it was known simply as 'Cheltenham', then 'Cheltenham St James' until 1925 when it came 'Cheltenham Spa (St James)'. Note, too, the ornate ironwork of the lamp post. *The Restoration & Archiving Trust collection*

CHELTENHAM SPA ST JAMES: The entrance to the station in May 1953 is awash with patriotic bunting celebrating the forthcoming Coronation of Her Majesty Queen Elizabeth II. Note the absence of traffic, with just a solitary Ford Popular parked outside the station. Note, too, the distinctive property standing behind the station to the right, which shows little change from when viewed in the earlier scene.

In St James Square today the large tree in the centre pinpoints the location of the station forecourt and entrance. Following the rundown of traffic, particularly after the demise of the old Midland & South Western Junction line from Andover and Swindon in 1961, and the GWR line from Kingham in 1962, the station finally succumbed to the inevitable and closed on 3 January 1966. Freight services delivering coal to the goods yard continued until October of that year. Although a new office block has replaced the house covered in ivy in the earlier scene, St Gregory's church and the distinctive property opposite still identify the old station's location. *Lens of Sutton/JW*

CHELTENHAM SPA ST JAMES: It looks to be a cool winter's day as steam oozes from BR Standard Class 5 4-6-0 No 73054 as it prepares to depart from St James with the 8.20am service to Bristol Temple Meads. The train is standing in the north island platform, with the spire of St Gregory's church in the background. A stabled rake of stock stands in one of the two sidings located between the two main island platforms of the station.

The scene today has totally changed, with no remnant of the station surviving. This view is from the service road at the rear of a Waitrose supermarket, which occupies a large part of the old station site. However, the building on the left is very similar to that partly obscured by the drifting steam of No 73054, which is believed to have been used as a school. *Restoration & Archiving Trust, John Dagley Morris collection/JW*

CHELTENHAM SPA ST JAMES: The first view was taken from a vantage point nearer the station building, as the distinctive roof spanning the booking hall can clearly be seen on the far right. On this occasion both sidings are occupied, as is the right-hand platform. Again St Gregory's church dominates the background. Standing in the platform on 22 September 1962 is GWR '5100' Class 2-6-2T 'Prairie' No 4163, which is about to depart with the 10.50am service to Kingham on the Great Western's Cotswold main line, via Andoversford, Bourton-on-the-Water and Stow-on-the-Wold.

Looking back into St James on 5 November 1960, the second picture reflects the progressive changeover from steam to diesel traction. On the left is Southern Railway 'U' Class 2-6-0 No 31791, about to depart with the 1.52pm service to Southampton via Andoversford, while in the adjacent platform is a DMU (later designated Class 119) bound for Cardiff.

A sports field and modern apartment buildings now occupy the station site, as seen from Jessop Avenue. Again the spire of St Gregory's church pinpoints the location. *Restoration & Archiving Trust, John Dagley Morris collection (2)/JW*

CHELTENHAM SPA ST JAMES: Services on the Midland & South Western Junction line had ceased by the time this photograph was taken in August 1962, and trains to Kingham would follow suit two months later. Standing in the platform is GWR '5100' Class 'Prairie' 2-6-2T No 4116 at the head of the 5.32pm working to Swindon. The background skyline is full of interest, with the distinctive spire of St Gregory's church on the left. The square bell tower on the right belonged to St Matthew's church, situated around the corner from St Gregory's, on Clarence Street. It was once the base for a spire, added in 1883 but removed in 1952 as it was deemed unsafe. The upper part of the bell tower, the section showing in this photograph, was removed in 1971. A smaller spire can be seen at the point where the base of St Matthew's tower intersects with the ridge of St Gregory's roof, which is attached to Cheltenham Library, while a third, more distant, spire is attached to Cheltenham Minster. *Kidderminster Railway Museum*

Opposite top: **CHELTENHAM MALVERN ROAD** station opened on 30 March 1908 some 21 miles and 3 chains from Honeybourne East Loop. It onsisted of a single island platform connected to Station Drive by a covered footbridge spanning the down line. A bay platform was provided at the north end of the down side where trains to and from St James could reverse. The station catered for through expresses, which all called at Malvern Road (the name of the road that crossed the line to the north of the station). It closed as a short-term wartime economy measure on 1 January 1917, reopening on 7 July 1919, but closed permanently on 3 January 1966 upon withdrawal of the passenger service. On the west side of the station were a raft of sidings serving the goods yard and an engine shed. Malvern Road West Signal Box was positioned just beyond the south end of the island platform, while Malvern Road East Signal Box was located between Malvern Road and St Georges Road bridges. Looking from track level, with the through avoiding line and some of the sidings in the foreground, GWR '6100' Class 2-6-2T No 6113 stands in the platform with the 5.00pm Gloucester-Cheltenham Spa (St James) service on 11 August 1965. Note the substantial brick retaining wall topped with iron spear-head railings.

The 'present-day' view is taken from what was the old island platform at a point roughly where the footbridge was positioned. The foot and cycle path uses the formation of the old down line through the site of the station, and there appears to be some of the platform brickwork and coping stones still in situ. However, a tall fence now portions off everything on the west side, where the old goods yard is now a building site for a new housing estate. The substantial retaining wall remains, as does a section of the spear-head fencing. *Kidderminster Railway Museum/ JW*

Below, right and below right: **CHELTENHAM MALVERN ROAD:** This undated picture was taken not long after the station opened, as staff, including the important-looking gentleman in the foreground, await the arrival of the approaching train. On the right is the driveway that leads to Malvern Road, with a horse and carriage in attendance next to the station entrance.

Nowadays the driveway from Malvern Road remains one of the main access points to the pathway, and this view shows how it has been extended over the space once occupied by the siding seen in the earlier scene. Note the wrought-iron pillar, which looks just like that positioned at the end of the railings, still attached to the retaining wall, seen in close-up in the third view. *Lens of Sutton/JW (2)*

CHELTENHAM MALVERN ROAD: Looking down from Malvern Road bridge towards the station on 22 August 1964, as GWR '4500' Class 2-6-2T 'Prairie' No 4564 departs with the final leg of an express from London Paddington to Cheltenham Spa (St James); the train will have previously reversed and been re-engined at Gloucester Central. Note the bay platform (seen above the first coach), now devoid of track since the withdrawal of the local service in 1960. Beyond, and to the left, is the station booking hall, positioned alongside the driveway to the station and just in front of the footbridge.

The same vantage point today reveals a completely contrasting scene, with just a path in place the running lines and abundant tree growth constricting the view. Still, the dogs seem to be having fun! *Tony Bowles/JW*

CHELTENHAM MALVERN ROAD: The south side of Malvern Road bridge is quite distinctive, as it looks to have either been widened or strengthened, or both, at some point. Approaching Malvern Road station is GWR '4500' Class 2-6-2T 'Prairie' No 4564 at the head of a Cheltenham Spa (St James) to Gloucester Central local on 22 August 1964. Malvern Road East Signal Box can be seen through the portal of the road bridge, and stabled just beyond is a Class 08 shunter with its distinctive yellow and back chevrons on the front of the cab.

Seen from a similar vantage point today, Malvern Road bridge remains distinctive, but now with the newer light-coloured stonework cleaned of the exhaust stains of steam locomotives. The jogger is approaching the location of Malvern Road East Signal Box, where the path, divides, with one spur heading into the site of St James station and the other along the course of the Honeybourne Line towards the site of High Street Halt and beyond. *Tony Bowles/JW*

MALVERN ROAD WEST SIGNAL BOX: This panoramic view from the embankment opposite 'Cheltenham Spa Malvern Road West Signal Box', probably taken in the late 1950s, shows a Swindon-built 'Inter-City' DMU departing. These DMUs were introduced from 1956 and were designed to cover express diagrams over shorter routes. Originally built for Edinburgh-Glasgow services, they were also used by the Western Region, particularly on services from Birmingham Snow Hill to Cardiff and Bristol. The 'A' headcode denotes an express passenger service, while a 'B' would indicate a semi-fast working. This scene also shows the extensive goods yard at Malvern Road, the coaling stage (centre) and engine shed (right).

By the early 1990s the scene has changed radically; gone are all the vestiges of the railway, and a DIY store occupies the land on which the goods yard stood. The only link between the two scenes is the gabled property, which can be seen to the right of the store and to the right of the engine shed in the earlier picture.

The land once occupied by the DIY store is now a building site for residential properties. The embankment from which the earlier shots were taken is now totally overgrown and impossible to access so this ground-level view represents an approximation of the site of Malvern Road West Signal Box, with the footpath following the course of the railway through the station site. *Peter Shoesmith/Geoff Dowling/JW*

LANSDOWN JUNCTION: The Honeybourne Line met the Midland Railway's Birmingham to Bristol main line at Lansdown Junction, which is just beyond the background road bridge. Closer inspection of the layout just beyond the left-hand arch of the bridge also reveals the junction with the line to Stow-on-the-Wold, which connected at Andoversford with the Midland & South Western Junction Railway to Swindon and Andover for Southampton; the latter closed to passengers in 1961, and freight from 1964 progressively through to 1972. Heading for Cheltenham Spa (St James) on 22 August 1964 with a service from Gloucester is GWR '9400' Class 0-6-0PT No 8471.

The location today, taken from roughly the same position, is part of Cheltenham station car park, and the route is effectively blocked by the large building that spans most of the space between the existing main line to Bristol and the trackbed of the Honeybourne Line. This building has the design of a motor car tyre and exhaust centre, but is actually a gymnasium with 'natural' air-conditioning, as the large front doors are open to the elements. Whether that still applies in winter remains to be seen! The brick retaining wall on the left remains the common feature between the two scenes. *Tony Bowles/JW*

LANSDOWN JUNCTION: An impressive signal gantry guards the approach to Lansdown Junction, located on the other side of the road bridge from which this photograph was taken. The bridge carries Lansdown Road itself, now the A40 trunk road, over the railway. The freight, hauled by War Department 'Dubdee' Class 8F 2-8-0 No 90346, is heading an engineer's train, judging by the consist of the wagons, and signalled for the Kingham line. These locomotives were ordered by the Ministry of Supply for use in various theatres of the Second World War, and more than 700 were purchased by BR soon after nationalisation in 1948. On the left can be seen the Midland Railway's Lansdown Road station. *Peter Reeves, Paul Dorney collection*

Opposite: **LANSDOWN JUNCTION:** It's a busy scene at Lansdown Road on 15 May 1982 as 'Peak' Class 45/1 No 45145 accelerates away from the station with the overnight sleeper from Glasgow Central/Edinburgh Waverley to Bristol Temple Meads. The train consists of Mk 1 sleeping cars, which were introduced between 1957 and 1964 and at this time were nearing the end of their working lives, soon to be replaced by the modern Mk 3 versions still in service today (new Mk 5 sleeping cars are due to enter traffic during 2019). Also passing through Cheltenham is a Class 37-hauled ballast train. By this time the Honeybourne Line track had been lifted, the scars of which can be seen on the right.

In the view from the parapet of Lansdown Road bridge in 2018 a brand-new Great Western Railway (formerly First Great Western) Hitachi-built Class 800/3 bi-mode unit, No 800308, curves out of Cheltenham on 22 July with a service to London Paddington. The new Class 800 units are gradually taking over the roles performed by the InterCity 125 High Speed Trains, which after more than 40 years in service are gradually being replaced, but not discarded, as other roles are being found for them. This view also shows the impact of the gymnasium on the trackbed of the Honeybourne Line. *Both JW*

LANSDOWN JUNCTION: In this view looking south from Lansdown Road bridge circa 1962, GWR '5100' Class 2-6-2T 'Prairie' No 4106 works a two-coach train off the Kingham line. Beyond can be seen the interweaving of lines where the former GWR and Midland Railway metals combine at Lansdown Junction itself. All this is controlled from the solid signal box on the left, which is of a wartime design and was constructed in 1942 when the route was quadrupled. It has reinforced walls and a concrete roof and is capable of surviving everything but a direct hit. In 1968 signalling responsibility for the Midland line passed to the new Gloucester Panel, but it retained control over the Honeybourne Line through to its closure in 1976, and was finally abolished in 1977; it survives as a Scouting HQ.

Looking over the parapet of Lansdown Road bridge now reveals a notably different scene. To begin with, an enclosed pipe now spans the formation just south of the bridge, which impedes the view towards Gloucester. However, Lansdown Junction signal box survives, although now partially hidden by the abundant lineside vegetation on the left. The newer building nearer the camera stands roughly where the Kingham line diverged. However, note that the distant footbridge remains. On 13 August 2018 two Arriva Trains Wales Class 153 DMUs approach forming a service from Maesteg to Cheltenham.

A second different viewpoint from Lansdown Road bridge provides a clearer view of the position of the closed Lansdown Junction signal box, and also well illustrates its robust construction, which was fitting for such a strategic location in wartime. It is, no doubt, as strong today as it was when first built. Passing on 13 August 2018 is an Cross Country Class 221 five-car 'Super Voyager' forming a service from Paignton to Manchester Piccadilly. *Peter Reeves, Paul Dorney collection/JW (2)*

Into Greet Tunnel. JW

Limited Edition — GWSR behind the scenes

The main part of this book looks at 'The Honeybourne Line' over the years, reflecting the history of the route in pictures. However, the Gloucestershire Warwickshire Steam Railway (GWSR) is a key component of any such history, and these additional pages reveal more of that railway, and provide a look behind the scenes to show how it operates. More importantly, it also reflects the people who continue to make it one of the most successful heritage lines. The GWSR is notable as being a volunteer-operated railway, with only a handful of paid, full-time staff. The voluntary aspect of its members and workforce has played a vitally important role in so many respects, from the early days of preservation and gradual expansion, through the dark days of the landslips to the triumph of the new extension to Broadway. This is truly 'The People's Railway'.

Acknowledgement

I would like to express my thanks to everyone at the GWSR for their help, understanding and patience in compiling this volume, and particularly these extra pages for the Limited Edition. My special thanks and appreciation must go to Graham Radband, the railway's Marketing Manager, who gave his time generously, arranged access to locations not normally available to the public, and also dealt with an avalanche of requests and queries from me over the past few months.

WINCHCOMBE Perhaps Winchcombe embodies the spirit of the railway, as the enterprise and tenacity of the volunteers created something really special in transporting, brick by brick, not just the old station building from the long-closed Monmouth Troy station, but also the former North Warwickshire Line signal box from Hall Green. In doing so, they created here the essence of a period Great Western station, which is now a joy to behold. Added to that is the sight of a former express passenger steam locomotive – withdrawn by BR in 1964, rescued from the breaker's yard in 1983 and the subject of a 33-year restoration project by volunteers – approaching the station at the head of a passenger train. The locomotive is former Southern Railway 'Merchant Navy' Class 'Pacific' No 35006 *Peninsular & Oriental S.N. Co.* JW

BROADWAY From nothing to something. This is the barren site of Broadway station in 2004, looking towards Honeybourne from a point near the road bridge.

After a period of 58 years, trains again operate into a completely new station at Broadway. The original station, opening in 1904, was demolished following closure in March 1960. Consequently, the GWSR had to start from scratch to provide a replacement. The new station follows traditional Great Western design and exudes atmosphere. This is the vision that everyone had dreamed of for decades, as the first train into Broadway, an engineer's working on 23 December 2017, stands in Platform 1 headed by Class 73 No E6036 with English Electric Type 1 (later Class 20) No D8137 at the rear. The permanent way team, who had closed the last gap in the track earlier that day, celebrate the occasion.

Finally we see the historic moment, just after 9.30am on Good Friday, 30 March 2018, when the first public passenger train for 58 years departed from Broadway, hauled by 'Hall' No. 7903 *Foremarke Hall*, and a new era for the GWSR begins. *Jo Roesen (2)/JW/Ian Crowder*

Below inset: The first Broadway tickets.

BROADWAY Eager photographers crowd the platform end on 21 March 2018 following the arrival of the first passenger train at the station for 58 years. *Jack Boskett*

Right: Behind the scenes at Broadway, as Booking Office Clerk Tony Stockwell takes a break between trains. *JW*

Below: The booking hall has a superb tiled floor and two impressive crush barriers protecting the ticket windows. That on the left is an original GWR pattern, while the barrier on the right is a perfect replica. Tony Stockwell looks on, awaiting his next passenger. *JW*

Right: Inside the new Broadway signal box, GWSR President Pete Waterman demonstrates his skills as a signalman at the launch of the April 2016 share issue aimed at providing the final funding for the completion of the new station. Work on commissioning the new signal box is ongoing. *JW*

Left: **BROADWAY** With the retaining wall in place, (left to right) Brian Thomas, Terry Andrews, Keith Selvin and Rod Whitcombe work on the task of back-filling the north end of Platform 2 in March 2015.

Centre left: A tug of war takes place between (left to right) Phil Boyer, Terry Boucher, Peter Kenealy, Keith Selvin, Dave Bowie, Robin Elliott and Gordon Wood and a large tree branch, which is being removed from the cutting alongside the north end of Platform 2.

Below left: This elevated view of the station site was taken from the roof of the new signal box. From left to right, Peter Kenealy, John Simms and Tony Boucher work on the roof trusses in March 2015. Note that the site for the new station building is being cleared in readiness for construction to commence.

Below: As seen from the recently installed centre span of the footbridge in July 2016, the steel frame of the new station building has been erected and bricklaying has commenced. *All Jo Roesen*

STANWAY VIADUCT is the most impressive structure on the line, and its 15 arches are now more open to viewing following the clearance of several trees at each end. No 7903 *Foremarke Hall* works hard away from the 10mph speed restriction with a Broadway-bound service. *JW*

Below left: This unusual view through the viaduct, looking south from a point beneath the first arch, shows that each pier has a central portal. *JW*

Below right: From the cutting south of the viaduct there is a clear view of the structure with D6948 approaching on a southbound train. *JW*

TODDINGTON is the headquarters of the GWSR, where the station buildings, signal box and goods shed all survived into the post-British Railways closure era. It is now also the home of the locomotive workshops for both steam and diesel traction. In this scene the joke is on the photographer, judging by the smiles on the faces of Station Master David Boot, and the footplate team on the DMU, comprising Steve Oddy (left) and Driver Ian Butler. The date is July 2012, when Toddington was isolated from the rest of the line to the south due to the Chicken Curve landslip. *JW*

Above: The station shop is situated on the up platform and carries a wide range of merchandise, including copies of this book – hopefully! Susan Edwards has control of the till, awaiting the next rush of customers. *JW*

Below: 'Behind the window' in Toddington's Booking Office are Booking Office Clerk Chris Matthews on the left and Station Master Andy Smith on the right. *JW*

TODDINGTON 'The Friends of Toddington Station' is a small band of people dedicated to looking after the station and surrounding area. It was formed nearly ten years ago, and now consists of more than 20 volunteers, some of whom travel considerable distances throughout the year to the twice-weekly working sessions.

Left: A long job in more ways than one, 'White Line Man' Andy Fogden keeps a steady hand while repainting the platform-edge white line. *Malcolm Nelson*

Left: 'A Pane of a Job': Malcolm Nelson begins the tortuous job of rubbing down the classic red telephone box prior to repainting. Only 72 panes of glass to work around! *Simon Pollock*

Below: 'The Powerwash Kid', Richard Evans, has a look of determination armed with his powerwash hose to sort out the accumulated grime on the station's footbridge. *Malcolm Nelson*

Below left: 'Saw Point': Mike Bailey demonstrates his woodworking skills on the platform, where normally he can be seen in his other role as station master. *Malcolm Nelson*

WINCHCOMBE 'Time to Go!' Station Master Barrie Etter checks his pocket watch before heading off with Station Assistant Mike Redhead (left) to meet the next train into Winchcombe. Booking Office Clerk Roger Thompson (centre) looks on. Barrie's pocket watch is no ordinary timepiece, but one presented to his grandfather by the London, Brighton & South Coast Railway for his services to the country in the First World War, during which he was gassed, wounded and awarded the Military Medal. He joined the railway as a signal box booking lad and rose in rank to deputy station master at Waterloo, where his duties included escorting HM The Queen and other dignitaries. *JW*

Winchcombe has an attractive booking hall, with a superb tiled floor. Railway artefacts adorn the walls, while Roger Thompson prepares to meet and greet new passengers at the booking office window. *JW*

WINCHCOMBE The former Monmouth Troy station building is split into three compartments, the booking office, booking hall and lastly a good-sized cafeteria, which also offers tables on the platform, and is a popular meeting place for both passengers and staff alike. Peter Groves and Vivienne Weston are seen in conversation with customers. *JW*

Enginemen at rest: after a busy morning operating a photographers' charter working with 'Manor' No 7820 *Dinmore Manor*, Train Guard Malcolm Hector, Driver Stephen Burnett (centre) and Fireman Clive Norton take a well-earned luncheon break, and are enjoying a good joke judging by their smiles. *JW*

GOTHERINGTON Since 1981 Bryan Nicholls and Savita Patel have restored the grandeur of the former Gotherington station, both in terms of the old station house and the adjacent goods yard. Although separate from the GWSR, there remains a close bond between them and the railway. Here Savita enjoys a ride along the goods yard siding on a velocipede. *Bryan Nicholls*

Maybe 'enjoy' is not the most appropriate word for the task in hand, as Bryan digs deep in order to replace a sleeper in the goods yard siding. *Savita Patel*

Right: **CHELTENHAM RACE COURSE** Many fascinating railway artefacts adorn the walls of the station booking hall, but actually the building itself is of significant historical importance, being the sole surviving example of a Great Western prefabricated structure, manufactured at Swindon and 'flat-packed' by train to Cheltenham. *JW*

Below: It is 'Ladies Day' at Cheltenham Race Course station, with Booking Clerk Sue White (left) and Station Master Teresa Black in charge of proceedings. *JW*

Below right: The booking office occupies the rear of the building, and is best described as long and narrow. However, conditions are not cramped, as seen here, with Booking Office Clerk Keith Norridge and Station Master Rob Davidson on duty. *JW*

Bottom right: The Race Course station shop and refreshment room is situated in the building on Platform 1. Here, sitting at the till position, Val O'Halloran welcomes customers with a beaming smile. *JW*

Above left: **ON THE TRAIN** On-train activity is all to often overlooked, with key roles performed unnoticed by passengers. But these roles are vital, as they probably have the most direct contact with the travelling public and thus are ambassadors of the GWSR. Guard Mel Curnuck stands in his compartment next to the hand brake wheel. He has the responsibility of ensuring the safety and operation of his train and passengers. *JW*

Above right: 'It's in here somewhere,' is the inevitable statement from the passenger trying to find his ticket for Travelling Ticket Inspector Geoff Hawkins to check. *JW*

Below: Judging by the smiles, there is a good joke doing the rounds. 'Passengers', actually Christine and Richard Hoy of the Catering and Permanent Way departments respectively, seem to have enlivened On Train Catering Steward Keith Warman's day. *JW*

Right: 'Bringing home the bacon': well, serving up the bacon buns actually, as Rosemary Radband delivers the much-anticipated sustenance to eager passengers. *JW*

Above: **LADIES** Heritage railways are traditionally seen as a man's world but, just like the 'big railway', women are increasing their presence, and ever more so in physically demanding roles. Here Angela Robotham is seen on the footplate of No 35006 *Peninsular & Oriental S.N. Co*, shovel in hand. She is presently designated as a 'cleaner' on the footplate, but is part of a training programme to become a fireman, and join two other ladies who are already passed for that role. How long until there is a lady driver? *JW*

Above right: Freehand sign-writing is an enviable skill on a heritage railway, where a tin of paint, a selection of brushes and a steady hand are much in demand. Such skills are well in evidence here, as Cheryl Newman of the C&W Department puts the final touches to the 'GW' logo on the side of a goods van. *Dave Clark*

Left: Putting her back into a physical job is Diana Barrell, as she tightens a fishplate bolt while working for the Permanent Way team. *Andrew Stratford*

Below: Annette Day is one of the happy band of Travelling Ticket Inspectors, who in addition to checking tickets also perform an important role in promoting the GWSR. *JW*

Right: **EVENTS** The Queen's Award for Voluntary Service (QAVS) is the highest award to local volunteer groups, which recognises outstanding work in the local community. In 2015 the volunteers of the GWSR received this award for their sterling work in supporting the railway. On 14 September Dame Janet Trotter presented the award to the volunteers, and is seen standing between (from left to right) Clive Norton, the late Alan Bielby (then company chairman), George Forrest and Jeff Lacey. *Jack Boskett*

Right: On 6 June 2017 Hayles Abbey Halt reopened, and received its first passenger train for 57 years following its closure in March 1960. Even the rain cannot damp the spirits of the small team responsible for the rebuilding of the Halt as they line up in front of GWR '1400' Class No 1450 and auto-coach in celebration of the event. *Jack Boskett*

Below: The official opening day of the extension to Broadway was Good Friday, 30 March 2018. Driver John Cruxon and Fireman Chris Smith stand with Chairman Richard Johnson and Lord Faulkner of Worcester with the plaque commemorating the historic event. *Ian Crowder*

DIESEL DEPARTMENT The GWSR can boast a varied fleet of diesel locomotives, which operate specific diagrams throughout the year. Their dedicated depot is next door to the steam shed, where the locomotives are both maintained and restored by a 50-strong team of volunteers. Here a problem had occurred with No D8137 preventing it from taking up its booked diagram, and owner Steve Madge (right) and second man Alex Raybould are actively engaged in rectifying the issue. Needless to say, the locomotive was soon back in action. *JW*

Right: Component recovery from the former Class 20 No 20305 (see page 53) is under way in the diesel depot, with the donor parts being used to keep No 8137 active. *JW*

Above left: **LOCOMOTIVE DEPARTMENT** This department occupies the David Page Locomotive Shed, and undertakes jobs from routine maintenance through to full overhauls and restoration projects. It can currently call on a team of 175 volunteers. 'What's this for?' Bob Mason might be asking, looking intently at a large nut that, judging by the even larger spanner nearby, is about to be connected to No 35006 *Peninsular & Oriental S.N. Co.* JW

Above right: In the inspection pit beneath No 35006 Steve Parker (left) and Paul Jenkerson look as though they are surfacing for air from the cramped confines of their work beneath the locomotive's leading pony truck. *JW*

Right: A team of three work on winterising the boiler of long-term resident BR Standard Class 4 No 76077. The 'smiley face' drawn on the wooden smokebox cover reflects that restoration work has commenced. Richard Winstanley (centre) takes a break from his role as Finance Director, and is aided by Mick Hobbs (left) and Jeremy Thomas, who is wearing the sinister face mask. Note, too, the headboards stored on the left. *JW*

Right: **LOCOMOTIVE DEPOT**
With No 7903 *Foremarke Hall* providing a backdrop, a team works on the leading pony truck of former GWR 'Heavy Freight' 2-8-0 No 3850, which is undergoing a major overhaul. Mark Harding (left), Chris Hayes, standing in the inspection pit, Martin Ginger and David Evans (far right) look to be in conference concerning the next task. *JW*

Below: A number of the heavy axleboxes from No 3850 are occupying the attention of Mark Young as he measures up for the next task. *JW*

Below: The Locomotive Department on their best behaviour, as seen in early 2018. *Tony Bowles*

Above: **CARRIAGE & WAGON DEPARTMENT** From the early days of working in the open at Toddington in 1982, the C&W Department is now located in the old goods shed at Winchcombe. Extensions in 2003 and 2012 greatly enhanced the department's capabilities to the point that it can now fully restore vehicles as well as maintaining the railway's operational fleet of coaches and wagons. The department now works four days per week and calls on an impressive pool of 111 volunteers. Here the disabled compartment in Mark 1 BSK coach No 21092 gets a top coat of paint courtesy of Ainsley Killey. *JW*

Above: The fitting of doors to the curved bodyside of coaches is not an easy task, and Peter Bennett (Department Head, C&W) has the task of testing the ease of opening of the guard's door, also on Mark 1 BSK No 21092. *JW*

Far left: Head of the C&W, Dave Clark (right), and George Rowland identify areas for the application of body filler on Mark 1 BSK coach No 34929. *JW*

Left: The enormity of the task of restoring vehicles is well illustrated as Dave Clark points to areas of significant corrosion at the end of a Mark 1 coach. *JW*

Above left: **CARRIAGE & WAGON DEPARTMENT** Phil Jones could be accused of 'just hanging around', but he is securely fastened to a safety harness while completing repairs to the roof of Mark I TSO coach No 4763. *Dave Clark*

Above right: The work bench displays an impressive array of tools necessary for the tasks ahead as Ken Reeves, Richard Stone and Paul Ellis work on Mark I TSO coach No 4986. *JW*

The railway has its own upholstery section, which maintains stocks of the various styles of seat covering, which are then machined to fit. Jenny Turner (left) and Penny Iron discuss a job in progress. *JW*

THE FOOTPLATE

Everyone is fascinated by the footplate of a steam locomotive, with all that pipework, the inferno in the firebox, the dials, knobs and levers. But it is the crew who attract the respect, attention and awe – they know how to keep this hissing, snorting metal monster in check! Once it was the dream of schoolboys to become engine drivers when they 'grow up', and although their ambitions may look in a different direction nowadays, the fascination with life on the footplate remains. A visit to the cab will always be the highlight of the day, and a memory for life. Driver Ben Evason has his hand on the regulator of No 35006 *Peninsular & Oriental S.N. Co* as he concentrates on the road ahead. The regulator governs the amount of steam being admitted to the cylinders, and therefore the speed of the train. The interesting notice above his head advises the driver that the locomotive is fitted with an overheating detector; a strong smell of garlic indicates that the inside big end is hot, and that specific action has to be taken to protect the locomotive. *JW*

Working on the footplate is not all sweetness and light; there are days when it can be downright unpleasant. Although the cab sheet has been employed, the crew of 'Manor' No 7820 *Dinmore Manor* are not fully protected from the elements as the rain swirls into the cab. Fortunately this service will operate chimney-first, as running tender-first in such conditions can be particularly unpleasant. Chris Brooks tops up his fire prior to departure from Broadway, as Driver Ian Windscheffel and Cleaner Tony Mace look on. *JW*

Right: **THE FOOTPLATE** The role of the fireman is both skilful and arduous. During a normal shift a few tons of coal will need to be transferred from the tender to the firebox, which certainly requires a high level of fitness. Dexterity is also required, due to the need to keep an even fire across the entire area of the firebox. The fireman's role also includes monitoring the water level in the boiler, as well as helping the driver by looking out for oncoming signal aspects. In the days of BR steam it was exclusively a male preserve, but nowadays the sight of a lady swinging a shovel is far from unknown.

Chris Blake looks to be feeding the centre of his fire as he launches a shovel full of coal into the inferno. Above him is the important water gauge glass, which indicates the level of the water in the boiler, and whether he will need to top this up. The boiler pressure is indicated by the dial to the right of the water gauge, which shows pressure of just over 200lb per square inch – the red line denotes the maximum of 250lb per square inch. Of course, the most important piece of equipment is the white billycan, brimming with hot, refreshing tea! *JW*

Above: It looks as though Driver Andrew Beale, seen leaning from the cab of No 5542, and Traction Inspector Jeff Lacey are having an interesting conversation at Cheltenham Race Course station, no doubt about the various nuances of enginemanship, and not the chances of the favourite in the 3.30 race! *JW*

Left: **THE FOOTPLATE** The working conditions on the footplate following the move from steam to diesel traction changed beyond all recognition. Instead of the cramped, dirty conditions of the steam footplate, Driver Richard Scott sits at the driver's desk of the GWSR's Class 117 DMU, enjoying all the comfort and protection from the elements it provides. *JW*

Below: Driver Tony Boston has the power handle of English Electric Type 3 (later Class 37) No D6948 as he runs around his train at Broadway. Note how spacious the cab compares with that of a steam locomotive. The other major difference is that nowadays there is no role for a fireman, or 'second man', as they were later known after the end of steam. *JW*

Above: **SIGNAL BOXES** Currently the GWSR has four operational signal boxes, at Toddington, Winchcombe, Gotherington and Cheltenham Race Course; work on commissioning the new signal box at Broadway is ongoing at the time of writing. Toddington is the only original signal box, which opened in 1904. Winchcombe signal box once stood at Hall Green on the North Warwickshire Line, while those at Gotherington and Cheltenham Race Course are completely new structures. At Toddington Signalman Saul Jones is in action as he energetically pulls over a lever to set the road for an approaching train. *JW*

Above right: Winchcombe's Duty Signalman Dan Rea is setting the road for an incoming service, and judging by his smile is very happy in his work. The former Hall Green signal box was dismantled brick by brick and re-erected at Winchcombe, ahead of recommissioning in 1987. It is often busy, as passenger services cross at Winchcombe requiring the signalman to leave his box to collect and exchange the tokens with both services. *JW*

Left: Cheltenham Race Course signal box is a more recent addition to the railway, opening in 2005. It stands in roughly the same spot as the original box, which was closed in 1964 and subsequently demolished. Dave Newman is the duty signalman, and is enjoying a 'busman's retirement', having previously been a signaller on the 'big railway'. *JW*

EXCHANGING THE TOKEN These classic views show a token exchange taking place at Gotherington. The first picture shows Fireman Paul Richardson on No 7820 *Dinmore Manor* with his left arm outstretched ready to collect the token for the section to Cheltenham Race Course. In his right hand is the token for the section from Winchcombe, which will be collected by Gotherington's signalman. The second picture shows the actual exchange; James Edwards, Gotherington's signalman, is wedged securely on his podium with his outstretched arm passing through the hoop of the token being offered by the fireman of No 7820, while the latter in turn scoops up the hoop for the section to Cheltenham. The knack is to keep a firm eye on the token to be collected, much like a sportsman keeps his eye on the approaching ball – a task certainly not as easy as it looks! Paul has now progressed to become a driver, while James also acts as a guard and duty operations manager. *Both JW*

EXCHANGING THE TOKEN There's a slightly different arrangement at Toddington. Here the DMU driver, eyes firmly fixed on the token, leans out of his cab window to collect it from Signalman Christopher Starr for the section to Winchcombe. In this instance, as the train has started only a few yards back in Toddington station, Driver Cliff Faulkner has no token to surrender. This task is probably more difficult for the driver, as he is having to control the DMU as well as secure the token, whereas in the case of steam the fireman would perform the task from the footplate, which also provided a higher vantage point. *JW*

At Winchcombe the token exchange is performed as the train enters the platform, as seen here with Signalman James Edwards offering the token onwards to Gotherington, or, if that signal box is switched out, Cheltenham Race Course. Note how the arm of Fireman James Clark on the footplate of No 7903 *Foremarke Hall* has hooked around the hoop of the token to firmly secure its collection. *JW*

Above: **THE PERMANENT WAY** The entire running line as well as the loops and sidings are managed by the Permanent Way Department, which operates two teams of highly skilled and experienced volunteers. Over the years they have laid and maintained the entire route, their most recent project having been the extension to Broadway. Because of the nature of their work they are hardy folk, used to working in all weather conditions. Here a JCB with a crane jib is being utilised to position a timber sleeper that will be the base for the northern loop turnout at Broadway. Head of Department Nigel Black supervises the operation. *Jo Roesen*

Above right: On a winter's day at Broadway in the rain, the team is laying a length of track within the confines of the new station. The person with the umbrella was probably very popular! *Jo Roesen*

Left: On another grim-looking day, weather-wise, the team drills holes for bullhead track chairs into jarrah wooden sleepers at Broadway. Two of the longest serving volunteers, Steve Long (left) and Jim Graham (right), look on. *Jo Roesen*

Below: A ballast drop at Little Buckland bridge causes a mini dust-storm as the wagons are slowly drawn along by the Class 73 locomotive. Three passing members of the team look on, probably unimpressed! *Jo Roesen*

Right: **THE PERMANENT WAY** Most of new extension to Broadway has been laid with continuous welded rail (CWR), which requires expansion joints to prevent it from buckling in very hot conditions. Here the team is installing such a joint at Pry Lane, at the end of the CWR section, after which, to maintain tradition, the track reverts to flat-bottomed rail and fishplates through to Broadway station.

Below: Not light work: sleepers are set down at Peasebrook Farm, four at a time, using two wooden spacers to maintain the correct distance between each. *Both Jo Roesen*

Above right: It is said that an army marches on its stomach. The permanent way team certainly does! The team takes lunch at Broadway, sitting on the rails they have just laid.

Right: The end is in sight: this is the view looking back at the end of a satisfying day with the recently laid track stretching out towards Broadway, whose former goods shed can be seen in the distance. *Both Jo Roesen*

Above: **THE SIGNAL & TELEGRAPH DEPARTMENT** (S&T) has just under 50 volunteers to call upon for the maintenance of the GWSR signalling system, added to which is the task of extending the system to include the new line to Broadway. The commissioning process of the new Broadway signal box is ongoing, with members of the S&T team seen working on the point rodding now in place. *Malcolm Walker*

Above right: Out of sight in the bowels of Broadway signal box, George Bryant works on connecting the locking frame to the signalling system. *Malcolm Walker*

Below left: **DRAINAGE** A small team looks after drainage matters, which is a significant problem due to the run-off of rainwater from the nearby Cotswold Hills – the landslips at Gotherington and Chicken Curve are testament to this. There are 76 culverts passing beneath the line, and it has been necessary to rebuild nearly half of them. Culvert 6B, near Laverton, was one of the major rebuilds, starting with Stuart Hamilton paddling in the flooded area while shovelling out silt in order to reduce the water level. *Alistair Watson*

Below right: Here is the nearly completed rebuild of Culvert 6B, with Roger Chandler (left) and Andy Protherough hard at work laying the final layers of brick. *Alistair Watson*

Above: **PEOPLE** Multi-tasking Richard Johnson strides along Winchcombe platform with a defective brake hose in hand. As a member of the C&W Department, he had just exchanged the offending item on a Mark I coach. When not attending to C&W matters, he is also a Travelling Ticket Inspector and a member of the Catering Department team, as well as filling the rest of his time as Chairman and Company Secretary of GWSR plc. *JW*

Above right: Paul Richardson, the driver of No 35006 *Peninsular & Oriental S.N. Co*, receives on-the-spot instruction on how to operate the new Broadway ground frame from Operations Manager Neil Carr on 22 March 2018. *JW*

Below: 'The Broadway Mob' look a determined bunch. Not to be trifled with are (left to right) Dennis Stevens (TTI), Roger Wyton (Station Master), Simon Taylor (TTI), James Edwards (Guard), and Ron Murray (Inspector). *JW*

Below right: Think twice about travelling on this train? A very spooky guard welcomes passengers onto a Hallowe'en Special. *JW*

Below: **COUPLES** The friendly atmosphere generated by the GWSR is reflected in the number of couples who are volunteers. 'Another bacon roll?' could be the question Rosemary Radband, of the on-train catering team, is asking husband and GWSR Marketing Manager Graham, who is well known for his love of such delicacies. *JW*

Above: 'I bet he doesn't buy anything,' could be John Wilman's aside to wife Sarah as their day as on-train catering stewards is interrupted by a would-be 'David Bailey'. *JW*

Below: Rod and Tina Whitcombe are another husband and wife team in their roles as on-train catering stewards. Their festive dress and broad smiles provide a clear indication of the time of year. *JW*

Left: Probably not the most likely place for a husband and wife team, but Diana and Dave Barrell are seen digging into the ballast as volunteers with the permanent way team. *Andrew Stratford*

Above: **THE NEXT GENERATION** The long-term future of the GWSR, like all other heritage lines, depends on its ability to attract young volunteers. It is good that the railway has seen some success in attracting new young recruits, including Saul Jones, who is one of a growing band of younger volunteers actively engaged with the GWSR. On this day he is Duty Signalman at Toddington, and enjoying the warmth of the pot-belly stove. *JW*

Above right: Another member of the young fraternity is Matthew Brown seen here in his role as a Guard, holding out the traditional green flag to indicate to the driver that he has 'right away'. *JW*

Right: Alex Caulfield displays a very steady hand as he refreshes the buffer beam number of No 4270 in the locomotive shed. He is also a member of the Carriage & Wagon team and, for good measure, a Travelling Ticket Inspector. *JW*

A Railway for all seasons. *JW*

List of Subscribers

List of Subscribers

Richard Abbey
John Aims
Richard Aldridge
Terry Andrews
Christopher Ashman
David Alyn Aspinall

Janet Baker
Desmond Baldwin
Joseph Harry Ball
Bill Ballinger
Philip Bannister
Kieran Barber
Brian Bartlett
Nigel Barton-Hawkins
Nicholas Bayston
Peter Charles Beard
Keith V. Beckett
Martin Beddall
Patrick Bedwell
John Berry
Frank Berry
Michael Beveridge
Michael Bickerstaffe
Jeanne & Gordon Boon
Tony Bowles
Phil Boyer
Pamela J. Brown
Roger Brown
Adrian Buckel
Alan Burton

Barrie Cartmell
Helen Carver
Roger Chandler
Brian Channon
Gary Cheetham
David J. Clark
Stephen Clark
Mr Nigel S. Clucas
Roger Coates
Richard Cockram
Peter R. Colville
Richard Cooper
Mr J.V. Crouchman
Ian Crowder

Phil Dalton
Rob Darby
David Davey
William Dawson
Anthony Delaine-Smith
Terry A. Dennison
David Dockrell
Mr Ian Douglas
Chris Dunn
Tony Dyer

Mr Brian Eddolls
Ted Ellis

4270 Winchcombe 22 April 2017

List of Subscribers

David Emms
Frederick Endsor

Darren Fairley
John Farncote
Stuart Farrimond
John Forkes
Stephen Francis
Paul Fuller

Mike Garratt
Mr D Gaston
Paul Gearey
Richard Giles
M. Ginger
Richard Glanville
Andrew Goodman
Graham Gould
Ian Grant
Peter Greaves
Mr A. C. Griffith
Dr Alan Groves
Mr J. C. Gupwell

John Haddleton
Ian Haley
John Hamer
Nicholas Hamer
Stuart Hamilton
David Hancox
Adrian Harding
Martin Harris
Marry Harris
John Harrod
Chris Haslewood
John Hawkins
Colin J. Hayton
Derek Headley
Mike Heath
Neil Herapath
Nicholas Hewlitt
Stephen Hill
Neil Hilton
Jim Hitchen
Phil Hobbis
Derek Holden
Colin Hollies

Mark Holman
David Holmes
Micheal Horwood-Smith
Nigel Hoskins
Christopher Howl
Michael Howse
Bavid Hucker
John C. Hughes
Raymond Hughes
Steve Hubin
Peter Hughes
Peter Humpheys
Robert Humpheries
Graham Huxley
George Huxley

Peter Jarmin
Kevin Jarvis
Mr Colin Jeacock
Meirion Jones
Saul Jones
Mr E. Jones

6023 *King Edward II* at Hayles Abbey 28 May 2018

List of Subscribers

Mr J.T. Kavanagh
Peter Kenealy

Chris Lane
David Lane
Peter Larner
Leslie Last
Fredric Leach
John Lewis
Mrs Eirian V. Lewis
John and Gill Lewis
Bob Lock
Alan Lovell
Michael Lowman

Erica Margreiter
Mr George Malin
Sue Marlow
F. G. Marsh
Neville Martin
Keith Martin
Jan Matthews
Chris Matthews
Ms. Karen McKenzie
MDS Book Sales
Brian Mead
Dr Alan Meakin
David Mendham
Bryan Merrett
Martyn C.W. Merrett
Maurice Miles
Derek Mills
Edward Minte
Roger Molesworth
Mr Keri Moreman
Richard Morris
Mr H Morton
Stella Mourant
Peter Muir
Neil Musgrove

Malcolm Nelson
Bryan Nicholls
Michael North

Derrick O'Brien
Ray O'Hara
Rev. David Oliver
Bryan Overbury

Kenneth Page
Barry Palmer
David Paterson
John Paul
John Pearse
Andrew John Peckham

D8137 Dixton Cutting 29 December 2015

List of Subscribers

Brian Penkey
Sam Perry
Patrick Phair
Geraint Phillips
Peter Phillips
Dave Palmer
Stephen Polley
Mr Graham Poole
Keth Porter
Philip Potter
Mike Powell
Sid Powell
Donald Prior
Jean Pullen
Alan Pye

Keith Quinell

Graham Radband
John Ragsdale
Peter Rawll
Alex Raybould
Peter Reddy
Mike Redhead
Stephen Reglar

Mr John Rendell
Dave Reynolds
Mr & Mrs M. C. Rhodes
Daniel Ridgeway
Keith Roberts
Jeff Robinson
Trevor Roderick
Phil Rogers
Carole Rose
Simon Roseveare
Michael Routledge
Peter Rowlands

Philip Salter
Dave Scott
Mrs B. Christine Sears
Jeremy Sellick
Chris Shilliam
Stephen Simmons
Peter J. Lippitt
Ian Sircombe
Christine Skelton
S. M. Skuce
David Slack
Bob Slater

Andy Smith
Andy Smith
Graham Smith
Malcolm Smith
John Spalding
Mr C. J. Sparks
Mike Speake
Chris Spencer
Paul Swift

Philip Taylor
Charles Thompson
Richard Tombs
David Tomlin
Jenny Turner
John Tyler
William Tyndall

Brian Vaux

Robin Walker
John & Rachel Walker
P. D. G. Wall
Richard Walton
Trevor L. Wand

7903 *Foremarke Hall* Gotherington 30 December 2018

List of Subscribers

Bruce Ward
Robin Ward
Richard Warner
David Wasley
Alastair Watson
Rod Wells
Revd. Peter West
Nicolas Wheatley
Anthony & Sandra Wheeler
Rod & Tina Whitcombe
S. J. White
Clive Whitwham
Mr Jeremy Wilkes
Ian Windscheffel
Richard Winstanley
R Woodcock
Howard Woodhouse

Alan York
Philip Young

Booksellers:

Ian Allan Bookshop (Waterloo)
Ian Allan Bookshop (Birmingham)
Bertram Books
Gardners Books
The Severn Valley Railway
Quayside Bookshop

Publisher's Dedication

The 'footplate crew' at Past & Present Publishing Ltd would like to place on record their appreciation of the enthusiasm and support that has been so much in evidence from all the team at The Gloucestershire Warwickshire Steam Railway in the preparation and production of this special Limited Edition volume.

The fact that the preserved sections of the railway are here to enable visitors to enjoy the feel of the steam age railway, is an amazing achievement. This represents and reflects the true spirit and ongoing hard work, dedication and determination of all those who are working to maintain and develop one of Britain's most outstanding railway experiences.

35006 *Peninsular & Oriental S.N. Co* Cheltenham Race Course 29 December 2018

Index

Past and Present

Locations

People